RIDERS ACROSS THE CENTURIES
Horsemen of the Spanish Borderlands

Riders across the Centuries

Horsemen of the Spanish Borderlands

Drawings and Text by José Cisneros
Biography by John O. West

TEXAS WESTERN PRESS

The University of Texas at El Paso

1984

Carl Hertzog, Consultant

Library of Congress Catalog Card Number 84-051461
ISBN 87404-089-2

Dedication.

Carl Hertzog
"pasó por aquí."

He glorified the printed page
in the land he loved so much.

J. C.

PHOTOGRAPH BY LUCY F. WEST

FOREWORD

The foresight, understanding and enthusiasm of Dr. Haskell Monroe, President of The University of Texas at El Paso, have made the publication of this volume a reality. His unwavering faith, assistance and encouragement have impelled me in the pursuit of my goal: a graphic depiction of the horsemen of our region down through the centuries.

Someone said that civilization came on horseback. This was certainly true of the culture and progress that originated in Europe and was brought to this continent with the arrival of the first equines in Veracruz in the year 1519. To follow their hoofprints along and across the land has been my objective. To restore, visualize and depict the physical appearance of their riders has been my aim.

Trying to reconstruct, to recreate, to retrieve from near oblivion the forgotten or very nearly lost characters that, at one time or another, roamed our land on horseback has not been an easy task. Years of searching in dusty nooks and remote places, leafing through worn-out papers and books and holding countless discussions with old friends have yielded the collection of types that comprise the subject matter of this book.

There have been many attempts at different times by different artists to graphically depict the history of horsemanship in Mexico and the southwestern United States. The difficulty in locating source material, the language barrier and probably the tediousness of the task have prevented them from succeeding. I like to think I had better luck and that my efforts will inspire future students to strive toward a greater knowledge of the subject through further investigation.

This present work is a greatly improved and extended version of my earlier book, *Riders of the Border*, published by Texas Western Press in 1971. My hope is that it will serve as a record as well as a guide to the collection of my original drawings acquired by The University of Texas at El Paso to be permanently displayed in the new library.

I wish to acknowledge with gratitude the help of those good people whose names appear below and to absolve them of blame for any errors of fact or interpretation that may have crept into the book despite our efforts to avoid them.

Through the years I have become indebted to many fine and talented persons for help and assistance in my endeavors. Several, I am sorry to say, have gone to their eternal reward. Those still with us and on whom I depend very strongly are: Dr. Haskell Monroe, pivot in this enterprise; Lucy and Dr. John O. West, super scribes; Carl Hertzog and Tom Lea, indefatigable advisers and consultants; Dr. Felix D. Almaraz, Jr. of San Antonio; Al Lowman of San Marcos, Texas; Dr. John Porter Bloom of Sacramento, California; Dr. Arthur Woodward of Patagonia, Arizona; Dr. Paul A. Rossi of Santa Fe, New Mexico; Sheila Ohlendorf of Austin, Texas; Dr. Marc Simmons of Cerrillos, New Mexico; and Dr. L. Tuffly Ellis of Austin, Texas, for much needed advice, assistance and research material. Special thanks go to Henry Schipman, Jr. of Las Cruces, New Mexico, who allowed me the use of his entire file on the Baja California *vaqueros*.

Those whom I greatly miss and who were of great assistance in the past are: Joseph Hefter of Mexico City; Randy Steffen of Dallas, Texas; Dr. & Mrs. J. Frank Dobie of Austin, Texas; and Lorence Bjorklund of Croton Falls, New York. And finally, my thanks and my love to my wife Vicenta, who cheerfully freed me from many of my household chores and other day-to-day obligations so that I might complete this task.

José Cisneros
March, 1984

THE ARTISTIC JOURNEY OF JOSÉ CISNEROS

Intended by the Lord to be an artist, an artist he became. . . .
— Lawrence Clark Powell

For sixty-five years now, José Cisneros has been striving for perfection in his art — beginning with his first youthful attempts at drawing a cow with a burnt stick on the adobe wall of his home in San Miguel, Durango. In the eyes of many, José has long since achieved perfection — but he has never become complacent. To him, his present best is a mark to be surpassed with his next effort — and his next.

That striving for the best, represented here in one hundred of the horsemen that typify his life work, has not followed an easy road. Nor were there many teachers en route to guide José. From very humble beginnings in a remote village near Canutillo, the retirement ranch of Mexican Revolutionary general Francisco "Pancho" Villa, José has made of himself an artist of international renown.

He has been honored repeatedly; he has been invited to show his work in many prestigious places. His drawings grace the walls of hundreds of homes; he is constantly sought after to illustrate books and articles — especially on the history of the Southwest. Yet he remains the gentle, unassuming family man, friend, citizen, and striving artist he has always been.

The future held little promise for the son of Fernando and Juanita Cisneros when he was born April 18, 1910, in Villa Ocampo, Durango (formerly San Miguel de las Bocas). Mexico was on the brink of the revolution that would keep the country in chaos for nearly a score of years, and keep the Cisneros family wandering from place to place during much of that time. José's mother's family were *vaqueros*, but the cattle business was precarious in those days. In Dorado, Chihuahua, Don Fernando found work as a carpenter, where his desire to make things beautiful as well as useful were limited by a scarcity of both tools and talent. He would do his best to improvise moldings with a handsaw, José recalls, and he maintained one link with tradition, making chests in the old Spanish way, with wooden pegs instead of nails.

During those turbulent times José taught himself to read with a phonetic primer, *Silabario Metódico*, memorizing the sounds of the letters and their combinations. An uncle from El Valle de Allende discovered that eleven-year-old José could read, and took him home with him for three years of schooling. There, in the town where, under its old name of El Valle de San Bartolomé, the expeditions of Espejo and Oñate in the sixteenth century had their starting points, young José met a teacher who made history come alive for him. His word pictures captured the interest of his pupil, and José recalls trying to imagine how the people of the past looked, how they dressed, how their horses moved and pranced. That fascination inspired by a nameless teacher was to have life-long effect on the artist-historian that José Cisneros was to become.

Desperate for pictures to aid his growing imagination, José appropriated illustrations from Sunday supplements in the newspapers used in a cousin's store to wrap groceries. At vacation time, José took his treasured papers with him on a visit to his parents' home. "But my parents didn't know what they meant to me. The next time I came back they had sold my collection for wrapping paper," José recalls.

It was during these days at his uncle's home that José first saw his art — and his words — in print. A household publication from Mexico City, *El Hogar* — the home — to which his uncle subscribed, contained a juvenile section, and at 14 José dared to send in a word sketch entitled "*Un Viaje*" — a journey — with a line-drawn self-portrait he had done at the age of eleven. The clipping, which José still has, has lost the lower part of the face, but luxuriant hair and intense eyes still remain as reminders of those early days. And what is even more interesting than the drawing is the subject of the essay: The journey is to school, where "his future teachers show him great fondness." The student completes his studies, proving his worth to his parents, teachers, companions, and *finally* to himself. "Thus must we all do, dear friends," young José concluded, "in order to triumph over the adversities of life." Such eloquence from one hardly more than a child exemplifies the determination that drove José Cisneros even then.

In January, 1925, the event was repeated: his second printed effort was "*Primavera*" — Springtime: a piece that has style, eloquence, and an attention to details of clouds and colors and flowers. An accompanying sketch shows a small lake at the foot of some hills, with trees and clouds. The overall effect, of words and picture, is happy and hopeful. It was indeed Springtime for José; the future was beginning to look brighter.

After three years with his uncle and attending school, José rejoined his family. Later in 1925 they moved to Ciudad Juárez, where Don Fernando found other work. José managed to get a school passport and enrolled in the Lydia Patterson Institute in El Paso, studying English especially, sweeping halls and classrooms to help pay his tuition, in addition to delivering newspapers mornings and evenings. His report cards show steady progress; in the 1927-28 school year he made straight A's in almost every subject. He was embarked on his own personal journey.

One summer he ran afoul of the immigration laws: during vacation he got a job in El Paso to help his family with their living expenses, but on a student passport that was taboo — so he lost his crossing permit. Herbert Marshall, director of Lydia Patterson, appealed to the immigration officials on José's behalf, and managed to get him a work passport so he could legally work in the United States. Since his schooling did not require homework, mornings and evenings were free for him to deliver his papers, do odd jobs, pore over his growing collections of newspapers and magazine illustrations — and he was free to concentrate on his own pictures. The family was not impressed with his early attempts at drawing, he remembers. "They just thought I was 'making *monos*'" — doodling, fooling around. But the spark kept burning, and despite the loss a second time of his collection of pictures — a brother borrowed them and didn't bring them back — he continued to practice his art.

In 1927 José cast his lot with the United States. In that year he "emigrated," although he continued to live in Juárez with his parents, bringing home whatever pay he could earn. His father was growing old, and José finally had to drop out of school and go to work full time to support the family. For about a year he delivered groceries in El Paso; then he got a job at the White House, a downtown department store, in the window-dressing department. One bonanza he discovered there was the used showcards from the window displays. "I would collect the old cards," he says, "because they were good on the other side. That's how I began my practice of drawing on posterboard."

Using the showcards from the White House, José developed an interesting technique: the posterboard had a clay coating, and José would cut through it with his pen for some lines, and with a wet finger or rag rub some of the area surrounding, producing a sort of half-tone/etching effect that was quite effective. This experimental method attracted the attention of a Mexican editor who wrote "He enjoys two techniques, that of the pen and of the half-tone. He dominates this double technique with ease and elegance." Such was the praise given by a man who would publish several of José's works. Nowadays, José points out, a drawing material called "scratchboard" is manufactured, to provide a surface for just this form of drawing — but José discovered the method on his own.

Cut off from the stimulation of school, José discovered another treasure — the El Paso Public Library and its world of books. For several years José haunted the library, gathering all the information he could from the books of history and art to be found there. His choices were guided in part by Maud Durlin Sullivan, director of the library, who had an intuitive power, it seemed. She knew just what was needed by a library patron. Miss Elizabeth Kelly, who worked with her for many years, recalls "She was wonderful. She could go down the shelves and show you the book that suited *you* best." José continued to study, and to draw, and began buying a few books of art for his own library.

The early 30s passed in this fashion, and finally José decided to try the magazines in Mexico City again. "I wanted to make a name for myself," he recalls. Another step on the "*viaje*" was at hand.

Although José's first publishing ventures did not bring him financial reward, the opening of magazines to his work gave him an audience that spread his name and his work far indeed — and doubtless gave him hope of something more tangible than just the thrill of seeing his work published.

That thrill, however, was quite intense for the young artist who saw his work on the cover of the Mexico City weekly *Revista de Revistas* in March of 1936. But this was only the beginning: over the next couple of years that magazine used four more of José's pictures for their covers. About the same time the monthly *Vida Mexicana* — Mexican Life — used a Cisneros watercolor, "Return from the Market," on its cover. And *Todo* brought together four of José's pictures on an inside page, together with a photograph of the artist.

But it was a new Juárez publication, *El León Juarense*, that really opened doors for José. There — again, for the experience alone — he illustrated poems, short stories, and articles. Then, about 1938 (to judge by the dates on the pictures) José began a series of "*Apuntes Históricos*" — Historic Notes — which he both wrote and illustrated. The first dealt with Cabeza de Vaca and his companions, the first Europeans to pass through the Southwestern region in 1536. Next in the series came the Rodriguez-Chamuscado expedition of 1581; that of Don Antonio Espejo in 1582; the *entrada* of Don Juan de Oñate in 1598; the founding of Paso del Norte in 1659; the construction of the Guadalupe Mission, 1662; and to end the series, a note on Colonial days in the area, 1750. The series is impressive, both for what it shows of the artist's developing style, and for the emphasis on history that has been a consuming passion in José's work for so many years. The details of costume and background are clear, precise, and completely true to the research sources available to the young artist-historian.

Then, in 1938 and 1939, an opportunity to reach audiences on the

"PIEDAD".—DIBUJO POR JOSE CISNEROS B.

Revista de Revistas
El Semanario Nacional

From a 1936 issue of *Revista de Revistas*, a Mexico City weekly, comes this magazine cover, evidence of José's early pencil technique.

northern bank of the Rio Grande presented itself. Lloyd and Hilda Burlingham began using José's work to illustrate, usually in full page form, short stories in their bilingual publication *The Mexico Magazine*. Again his subject matter is Southwestern, and often with a historical scope in costume and detail. He did one cover, depicting the front of the *Palacio Nacional*, the seat of government in Mexico City, at the moment of a formal event such as the annual re-enactment of the *Grito de Dolores*, the call for independence of Miguel Hidalgo y Costilla. And for a bonus, José was paid for his work; it was only four or five dollars per drawing, but he had reason to feel that good things were on the way!

About this same time José's work appeared in *El Correo de Parral*, illustrating a poem, "Basuchil: Un Romance de Tierra Fría." The author was Heriberto García-Rivas, a fellow member with José in *El Ateneo Fronterizo* — the border Athenaeum — a local organization of artists, poets, and authors who met together to share matters cultural. The association was a flattering one to the young artist, being accepted as an equal with people who had attained success. His talents made him welcome, and one member of the group, Federal District Judge Miguel López Schoeffeger, offered to send José to the Instituto de Bellas Artes in Mexico City to study art formally. However, his mother cried and swore she would never see her son again, so he stayed at home. Several times he was asked to illustrate the works of his associates, including another García-Rivas poem, "Teporaca," which was published in Mexico City, that celebrated the Tarahumara Indians of Northern Mexico. José's illustrations are strong, virile depictions of these hardy people, a bit romanticized, but vivid with detail nonetheless.

In 1937, encouraged by his Mexican publications, José took another important step on his journey. Tom Lea, a well-established El Paso artist, was painting a mural at the United States Courthouse, depicting the giants who had come through the Pass of the North. José watched the work grow, and then one day he brought a sampling of his work to show Tom Lea. The result was gratifying indeed. Mr. Lea seized a piece of tracing paper and wrote the following note that was to have a powerful impact on the young artist's life.

Addressed to the librarian who had helped José earlier with his studies, the note read:

Mrs. Sullivan —
  This will introduce Sr. Cisneros, who has just come into the lobby of the Court House, to show me his drawings — which I think are EXCEPTIONAL — I thought you would like to see them, and perhaps exhibit them. This fellow has some stuff.

Regards
Tom Lea

José's first El Paso show exhibited 40 drawings in the El Paso Public Library. Most were pen and ink, with a few in color. Costumes and figures revealed the artist's interest in the Spanish and Mexican periods of Southwestern history. The *El Paso Herald* reviewer commented on the artist's "remarkable skill" in depicting an Aztec, a *padre*, a "French soldier in baggy trousers and Maximilian on horseback." Tom Lea commented positively on the exhibit, as did many library visitors. The exhibit was such a success that it was extended from one to two weeks. One hoped-for event, however, did not come to pass. Mrs. Eleanor Roosevelt was coming to El Paso the first week of March, 1938, and her schedule called for a visit to the library. José told Mrs. Sullivan "If Mrs. Roosevelt likes my drawings, she can have any one she wants." But the visit did not materialize, else the work of José Cisneros might have hung in the White House in Washington many years before his works first appeared in that city.

One of the reviewers of the exhibit was the poet Heriberto García-Rivas, whose praise was powerful indeed. "José Cisneros Barragán is young and Mexican," he wrote, "which is to say dynamic and artistic by heritage." He went on to comment on the hours of labor that had gone into the drawings, and marveled at the eloquence of the pencil or pen in the agile fingers of the young artist. His drawings "have the pure air of the heights of the viceregal era, the rare atmosphere of the central highlands, the limpid heavens of the valley of Anahuac,

A gift to the El Paso Public Library, where José Cisneros' first public showing was held, is a "Thank-you" that includes the people of earlier times who came to the Pass of the North. Used as the official library bookplate, it is reproduced through the assistance of Mary Sarber.

which absorbed, without destroying it, a complete and ancient civilization." Such praise of his first North American showing must have been almost overwhelming to the artist. There was more to come.

Before the end of March the exhibit had been transported to the neighboring city of Juárez. The Centro Escolar Benito Juárez, to inagurate its new auditorium, held not only an *Exposición de Arte* by one José Cisneros, but produced a gala affair — artistic dancing, solo and twin piano presentations, vocal music, and poetry recitations. Also included was an introduction and analysis of the artistry of the young José by Armando B. Chávez, director of the school and member of *El Ateneo Fronterizo*. At the end of the exhibit, Sr. Chávez wrote a penetrating review that is similar to what art critics of the 1980s have to say, praising the minute, careful details of José's work, his originality, spiritual qualities, the deep sentiments and constant artistry at work in dealing with people, costumes, and scenes from the historic past. All this, Chávez predicted, "augurs a complete success in his career."

The meeting with Tom Lea had another powerful impact on the career of José Cisneros. Tom had been working with Carl Hertzog, artistic book designer and typographer, since 1935, and hoped that José's work might also find a welcome in the projects of the day. The first opportunity was a modest one. When Rabbi Martin Zielonka of Temple Mount Sinai passed away, the El Paso Rotary Club and the Inter-Religious Good Will Association of El Paso (forerunner of the local chapter of the National Conference of Christians and Jews) asked Mr. Hertzog to prepare printed memorials in honor of the rabbi. With fine deckle-edged hand-made paper and hand-set type by Carl Hertzog, the documents were set off with style in the form of illuminated initials, highlighted in red — the work of José Cisneros. The year was 1938; several years would pass before the first major collaboration of the three men.

The late 1930s were busy ones for José. He continued working at the White House Department Store, drawing in his spare time — especially horses and horsemen — and studying his art. Don Fernando died in 1939, leaving José in charge of his mother's welfare. Also in 1939 José acquired his most loyal supporter and helpmeet, Vicenta Madero. Between them they raised five daughters and a niece, and they became collaborators in José's aspirations as well. José explains how this cooperation came about: "One of the tragedies of my life is to have been born color-blind. In order to properly color a picture I have to see the name of the color. Otherwise, if I take it at random, I may take brown instead of red or green. In the beginning I mentioned this to Tom Lea, and he told me not to worry about it — that I had a world in itself in black and white." Still, people love color, and José has used water color and colored pencils to add richness to his already impressive pen and ink creations — and Vicenta, who has a very good eye for color, usually advises him. To see one of José's richly dressed church or government officials or military men, with elegant bridles and saddles and other gear, resplendent in their vivid colors, is to agree that this husband and wife team complement each other beautifully. José says he enjoys using color very much, even if he has to go by the names of the colors on his pencils. "The funny thing is, I get a lot of compliments from people for my use of color, and I have to laugh inside!"

During the 1940s, with war clouds gathering, José took a course in aircraft sheet metal work, and even had a job waiting in a California aircraft plant — but the responsibility for his mother, and Vicenta's reluctance to leave El Paso, kept him from taking on the new profession. Instead, he went to work at El Paso City Lines, a job that was defense-related. He remained with the firm until his retirement in 1973, rising to foreman of the painting division — and creating some of the most colorfully decorated streetcars in the world, especially those on the El Paso-Juárez line with their displays of flags of the border states of two nations. Although an occasional job for Carl Hertzog arose, it was a quiet time for his artistic growth.

Much has been said of the individuality of José Cisneros' art, the fact that he is self-taught, that he had no artist-confidant during his early years. He had to work out his artistic problems alone — but in the printed page he had found some clues as to their solution.

Way back in El Valle de Allende, as he once told me, he had no basis for visualizing the historic characters and events his teacher described. He tried to capture these images on paper, but he simply did not know how! Had his development stopped there, the world might have had another so-called naive or vernacular artist of the schoolboy variety. But early he found kindred souls to learn from.

One of the first was Alejandro Sírio, an Argentinian. "He did beautiful work; he was an authority on Spanish costumes, and executed them with emphasis on strong outlines, only a little stylized," says José. "I tried to follow his style, in a way. I also admired a Mexican artist, Ernesto García Cabral. He was very prominent in those days, a great illustrator, but he has been forgotten now. I had several reproductions of his work in my collection of newspapers that was sold." Americans Norman Rockwell and Howard Pyle also helped form the artist's taste. José recalls that Rockwell, especially with his *Saturday Evening Post* covers, was the first available example of American artistry for study. And since the *Post* cost only five cents in those days, it was inexpensive to study Rockwell's realism, his draftsmanship, and his American themes, all of which were most

The 17th-century gentleman (above) and 18th-century nobleman
(at right) were drawn by Cisneros as costume designs for an early
El Paso Sun Carnival theme. Later, they were purchased for six
dollars each by Dr. John W. Cathcart — and were Cisneros' first
individual sales. Reproductions here are through the courtesy of
Florence Cathcart Melby, Dr. Cathcart's daughter.

impressive. José considers Pyle the father of American illustration — "He illustrated everything, from children's books on up," José explains. "I was fascinated by his style. He did good color work, but I really liked his pen and ink drawings; then I developed my own way, different from what Pyle did."

José obviously is not the product of any "school" of art; although he has sampled the works and techniques of many individual artists, he is quite selective. And, like the giant that New Mexico historian Marc Simmons insists he is, he has gone his own way and developed his own tastes. On matters of art and history he can be very forceful. One afternoon after we had been talking about this book, and his earlier *Riders of the Borderland*, where I had quoted him on a mild note of disapproval of artist Diego Rivera, José telephoned me to clarify his views: "Diego distorted his figures as much as he distorted Mexican history," he told me — and repeated it while I wrote it down. I could almost see his black eyes sparkling as he spoke. Anyone familiar with the lives and works of the two men will appreciate the strength of feeling behind this incident.

Because this book represents the culmination of my lifetime ambition, I dedicate this No. 1 copy to my beloved, devoted and ever loving wife,

Vicenta,

who has shared with me the joys and sorrows, anxieties and happiness of almost half a century together.

Lovingly,

José

The beauty of José's calligraphy, the simple eloquence of his book dedications, and his recognition of and love for his wife Vincenta are united in this reproduction from the flyleaf of Copy Number 1 of *Riders of the Borderlands.*

The calligraphy that José Cisneros does so well — one critic said his was the most beautiful in America — is particularly prized in a personal letter or an inscription in one of the many books he has illustrated. But again, the art was self-taught. He began by drawing each letter, a slow and laborious process; then one day he discovered a book on the subject, and came to realize that certain strokes were made a certain way. Then he realized why certain calligraphic effects worked so well.

Much later José tried, one time only, a mural on a plaster wall. Francis Fugate, an El Paso author and teacher who wrote the text for one of José's most important works, *Our Spanish Heritage*, asked him to create a mural on his garden wall, a scene suggested by the drawings from the book. "José worked out his own method of painting the mural," Fugate said, "and then we found that it was exactly the same method Michelangelo used!" The instincts of a genius must have been at work!

Joseph Hefter of Mexico City, a recognized authority on military costumes, was a great help in directing José's research in that area — one quite necessary for the artist who would accurately portray horsemen, especially military horsemen. And that knowledge led to a commission to do scenes of social and garrison life for the Fort Bliss Officer's Club (as well as a commission years later to do a series of horse soldiers for the State National Bank at the post). When the first series was presented, José recalls, it was the occasion of the dedication of the Fox Room, honoring "Mr. El Paso" Chris P. Fox, long-time community relations liaison between the United States Army and West Texas. Not many years before, Vicenta had worked as a maid in the quarters of a captain's family at the post. She and José were engaged, but the Depression and José's small earnings made marriage impossible for a time. José would ride the Fort Bliss street-car to the end of the line, just outside the military reservation, to wait for Vicenta to get off work. After finances improved and they could get married, Vicenta stayed busy with home and family. Now, on this important occasion, José and Vicenta were both invited to the presentation dinner, and as persons of honor were seated at the head table, Vicenta beside the commanding general, at his request. Carl

Hertzog, seated among the many city and army notables present, thought "They've got it made!" But José and Vicenta could only feel grateful at how times had changed for them in a few short years. Such gatherings, and such honors, have become quite frequent; Vicenta is always present; her quiet charm and poise radiate, whatever the occasion.

Other challenges over the years have found José ready to meet them. He drew the designs for a new technique in stained glass, that El Pasoan Ralph Baker worked out for the B. M. G. Williams Hall at St. Clement's Episcopal Pro-Cathedral. Between them they produced 23 stained-glass windows where the picture can be seen from both sides. José designed the stations of the cross at St. Joseph's Church, where he and Vicenta worship, and Father William Ryan had a wood craftsman carve them. Later José designed two plaques for the Immaculate Heart of Mary Church in Las Cruces, New Mexico, but the wood carver did not follow the design, so the artist acquired some woodcarving tools and did the job himself. "It's like making a drawing," José said, "only it takes more time because I'm not familiar with the method of woodcarving. But little by little. . . ." Later he carved a crucifix for Father Ryan's new St. Matthew's Church, and designed another for St. Genevieve's church in Las Cruces.

Another area in which José has worked is the carving of plaster masters for the molding of bronze plaques. Several examples of his work in this medium adorn public buildings in the region. One, memorializing the straightening of the Rio Grande channel in a cooperative venture of his native country and his adopted one, graces Scenic Point on El Paso's Mount Franklin, where one can look down at the river and follow the details shown in the plaque. José has designed countless letterheads and bookplates, logos for organizations, and similar works of art. One of the most striking — and one that brought together the talents of Hertzog, Lea, and Cisneros — was the seal of Texas Western College.

During the presidency of Dr. Wilson H. Elkins, it was made known that Texas College of Mines and Metallurgy was about to be given a new name. Graduates felt uncomfortable, Dr. Hertzog says,

This study was done for a crucifix for St. Genevieve's Church in Las Cruces, one of many gifts to area churches by José Cisneros.

at receiving a degree in music or art or literature from a mining school. Since the previous seal featured a pick and shovel, a new one befitting the new name was needed. Tom Lea had done a design earlier of the Rio Grande flowing between two mountains, and with his approval Hertzog and Cisneros put their imaginations to work on the idea. After Carl had expressed approval of the aritst's design, Carl began experimenting with colors to get the right shade of land and sun and sky. And years later, when the name of Texas Western was changed to The University of Texas at El Paso, the seal was adapted by José to accommodate the new name. Significantly, all three seals now grace the front of the new library building where the original drawings of the horsemen in this book are to make their permanent home.

The seal of Texas Western College features the Pass of the North, and the Lone Star of Texas, and also represents the collaboration of José Cisneros and Carl Hertzog.

The versatility of José Cisneros' artistry is inspiring indeed, but the major thrust of his career for quite some time was guided and encouraged by his association with Carl Hertzog, the man J. Frank Dobie called "printer without peer between the Atlantic and the Pacific." In 1946 Hertzog was producing a program for National Music Week in El Paso. Seeking to avoid what he regarded as the cheapening effect of columns of advertising used to defray expenses, Hertzog found a sponsor in Dorrance D. Roderick, and filled the unused advertising spaces with biographies of American composers.

Available pictures of the composers were so varied that he asked José to make uniform sketches for what was the first major collaboration between the two men.

The next year when Hertzog was working with Everett de Golyer, preparing a facsimile reprint of the story of three shipwrecked sailors whose journey had been told in Haklyut's *Voyages*, he was discussing the project with Tom Lea. Tom said Carl needed "some wire-edged drawings, some sharp pen work." As if it were ordained, the next day José Cisneros walked by Carl's shop and was called in. The printer asked the artist if he was still doing his pen and ink drawings. "I said yes, I was still practicing," José recalls. "The next day I brought the portfolio I had been working on, and he thought it was just the type of drawing he needed for the book." Mr. de Golyer didn't like the first frontispiece José drew, so Tom Lea suggested he reduce the size of the three wanderers, having them dominated by an immense sky. José's second trial, following Lea's suggestion, was accepted for the frontispiece — but Hertzog, who liked the first version, used it on the dust jacket. The result, *Across Aboriginal America: The Journey of Three Englishmen Across Texas*, is a classic, one that José considers to be his most prestigious early publication. And book lovers agree with him: a collector recently paid $195 for a copy of it.

The book also got José started on another of his specialties, making maps. Over the years his maps, with distinctive additions and decorations, have enriched scores of books of the West and Southwest. Yet, curiously enough, José does not like to do maps! They limit his artistic imagination, he says, in that he has to stick to the "facts" of the terrain. "It's very boring trying to get things into a certain place. I've been used to doing my own work, without copying either from life or anywhere. Drawing on my own imagination, I can change things — put more shadows on this side or that, making my own likeness. That's why I'm not a portrait artist. . . . You have to rely completely on the model, otherwise it wouldn't be a portrait. In such works as the Halsell book [W. C. Holden's *A Ranching Saga*] I copied photographs, but I could select those things I wanted to stress, or change the background, like the one I did for Al Lowman's *Printer at the Pass*. He supplied me with a photograph of

Reproduced here is the frontispiece of a classic, Everett de Golyer's *Across Aboriginal America*, considered by José to be his most prestigious early publication.

A photograph by Sue Flanagan was the basis for this portrait of Carl Hertzog for the 1972 bio-bibliography *Printer at the Pass* by Al Lowman, who gave permission for its use here.

Carl Hertzog, but I arranged to have Mount Franklin in the foreground, and symbols of early printers, like Johann Gutenberg and Aldus Manutius, in the background." José also, appropriately, used Carl Hertzog's own identifying emblem.

The association of Cisneros and Hertzog soon resulted in another quality production: *The Red River Valley, Then and Now.* The work was made up of columns by Alexander H. Neville, the South's oldest living journalist at the time (1948), and each segment had a distinctive Cisneros sketch at its head. The endpapers and dustjacket presented a masterpiece: a Cis-

neros map of the Red River region, floating like a cloud above a long scene of the river itself, and the huge "river raft," a log jam that for decades blocked the main channel and impeded navigation. Carl Hertzog sees this book as a landmark for José, since it was his first work involving non-Hispanic subject matter in any quantity, and showed clearly the range of his abilities.

The year 1948 saw the success

This section adornment is from Cisneros' first non-Hispanic work — the illustration of A.W. Neville's *The Red River Valley, Then and Now,* Paris, Texas, 1948.

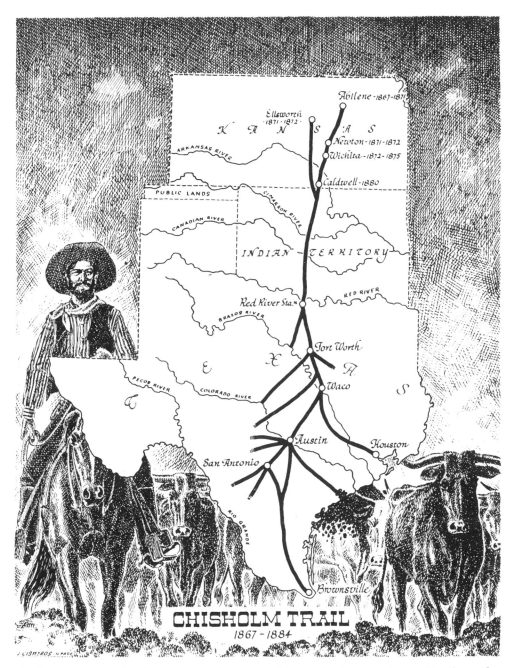

A Cisneros map is always something special, as is this one from *Trailing the Longhorns* by Sue Flanagan, published in 1974 by Madrona Press. It appears through the courtesy of editor Clois W. Bennett.

of another cooperative venture by Hertzog and Lea that concerned José Cisneros. The two men served as unofficial sponsors for the naturalization of the artist from Mexico. Ironically, despite their friendship and support, they could not serve as official sponsors: Carl had been born in Lyons, France, while his father was studying music there; and Tom had too recently been out of the country, during World War II — so José's foreman and a fellow worker at El Paso City Lines were his official sponsors. The "adoption" of the new nationality for José was now official.

The very next year came another Hertzog/Cisneros classic, Cleve Hallenbeck's *The Journey of Fray Marcos de Niza*. Named by the American Institute of Graphic Arts among the Fifty Books of the Year, the work also won for José his first award: Best Illustrations by a Texas Artist, given jointly by the Texas Institute of Letters and the Dallas Museum of Fine Arts.

Another combination of talents and events produced *The Spanish Heritage of the Southwest*. It began with the search for a theme for the 1951 *Flowsheet*, the yearbook for Texas Western College. Because of the school's location, and its large proportion of students of Hispanic origin, Hertzog proposed "Our Spanish Heritage," and with a cover and twelve division pages by José Cisneros, a distinctive annual was created. The following year, with augmented text by Francis Fugate and the addition of a map of the area by José, the first publication of Texas Western Press came into being, using the masterful artwork that had appeared in the yearbook. Even the cover of the book was a new departure: it was printed from the surfact of an adobe brick, a distinctively typical symbol of the Spanish Southwest. As José recalls the event, "My leanings have always been toward the Southwest. The Spanish Heritage, I think is one of my best accomplishments of all time."

Not all Hertzog/Lea/Cisneros ventures have borne such fruit. In the early 1940s Maud Durlin Sullivan gave Carl Hertzog a deluxe edition of the story of Cabeza de Vaca, done by Grabhorn Press. Carl and Tom Lea decided they could do a similar deluxe edition of the work of someone else who had been a part of El Paso history.

Mrs. Sullivan made a bibliographic search and reported that the

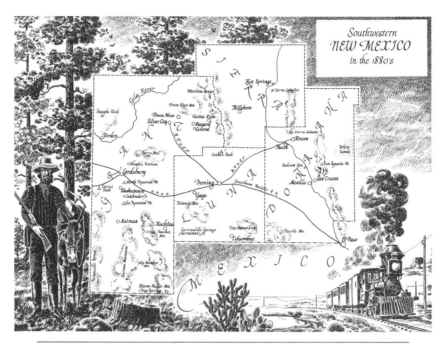

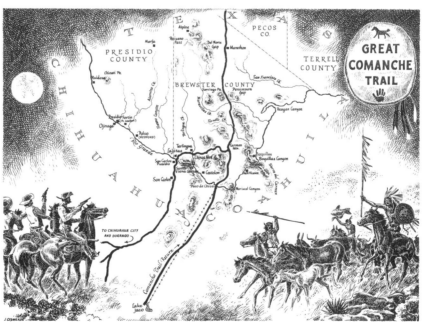

A Texas Western Press book, O.W. Williams' *Pioneer Surveyor, Frontier Lawyer*, had these Cisneros maps to help orient the text.

Coronado expedition was available for such a venture. Tom made some drawings, Carl set a page of type, and José brought in a scene for possible inclusion — but then Mrs. Sullivan burst the balloon: under the name *Vasquez de Coronado* she discovered that there *had* been a deluxe edition published, so all the planning came to naught.

Over the years scores of works produced by Carl Hertzog have been enriched by frontispieces, maps, dust jackets, and illustrations by José Cisneros. Included are such books as *El Sal del Rey* by Walace Hawkins; *The Typical Texan* by Joseph Leach; *Tales of the Tularosa*, Mrs. Tom Charles; *The Mezcla Man*, J. Frank Dobie; *Bells over Texas*, Bessie Lee Fitzhugh; *The El Paso Salt War*, C. L Sonnichsen; *Morelos of Mexico*, Wilbert H. Timmons; Eugene O. Porter's *San Elizario: A History;* and Sonnichsen's *Pass of the North*. Also produced were dozens of Southwestern Studies, issued by Texas Western Press under covers that bear a map of the region by José Cisneros. In addition, two of the monographs in the Southwestern Studies Series featured Cisneros work: Number 30, *Riders of the Border*, a selection of thirty of José's horsemen, and number 52, his *Faces of the Borderlands*. The latter was designed by Hertzog's successor as director of the TW Press, Evan Haywood Antonne, and cel-

Joseph L. Leach's *The Typical Texan*, SMU Press, 1952, had this evocative frontispiece and dust jacket illustration.

Bishop Juan de Zumarraga and Mexico's first Viceroy, Antonio de Mendoza, brought the first printer, Juan Pablos, and the first printing press to the New World. This illustration appeared in *Our Spanish Heritage*, the first publication of Texas Western Press, in 1952. The original is reprinted through the courtesy of Elka Tenner.

ebrated the twenty-fifth anniversary of Texas Western Press as its 130th publication. The book was dedicated by the artist "To Vivian and Carl Hertzog with gratitude." Text and drawings in these works brought José full circle, to work he had begun many years before, when his series "*Apuntes Históricos*" had allowed him to provide both words and pictures out of his historic research. A more recent book, *Riders of the Borderlands*, published by the Centennial Museum at The University of Texas at El Paso in 1981 and designed by Carl Hertzog, displayed vividly the growth and the mastery of his art by José Cisneros since those early days.

The encouragement and the exposure given to José and his art by Carl Hertzog have had some interesting results. One of the most memorable goes all the way back to *The Red River Valley* in 1948. The book was to be presented to the author, A. H. Neville, on the occasion of his 85th birthday at a celebration in his hometown, Paris, Texas. Carl and José drove the long way together, discussing printing, art, and life in general. The birthday was a big event for José, and he enjoyed greatly the prestige and attention he received for his illustrations. On the way home, Carl drove by Austin, where José was introduced to Miss Fannie Ratchford, curator of the rare books at The University of Texas Library. Miss Ratchford's nephew took José touring while Carl and the librarian talked business, and José came back with his eyes sparkling: "I've just met Dr. Castañeda!" Carl says he thinks José could not have been more excited if he had just encountered the King of Spain. Out of that meeting came an opportunity for José to illustrate Carlos E. Castañeda's fifth and sixth volumes of *Our Catholic Heritage* and several other works. Robert Frost once wrote about "how way leads on to way. . . ," and such has been the case with José and his interconnected contacts with historians and authors and lovers of art.

One case in point arises concerning a map José once reproduced in *San Elizario*. The original was by Don Bernardo de Miera y Pacheco, who about 1776 came through the Pass of the North and recorded it on a map. "He was probably the first real artist who came through this part of the country," José says. "He was artist, sculptor, and painter, working in both color and black and white." José found his map to be memorable, and did an interesting interpretation of it. Recently Bud Newman, one of the guardians of the Hertzog Collection at the UT El Paso Library, came to José for help with a research problem. A number of writers had been seeking the location of Las Caldas — a long extinct settlement in the area of the Pass, mentioned in several documents in the Juárez Archives. José pulled out his copy of the Pacheco map and pointed the site out to Bud — and Bud then shared the information with other interested historians.

The association of José Cisneros with Dr. Castañeda led to another fulfilling contact: Fray Angélico Chávez, OFM, another of the most prominent Hispanic historians of the Southwest, called on the talents of Cisneros for several of his books. In a presentation copy of *The Missions of New Mexico*, Chávez wrote "To José Cisneros, who should have been the illustrator of this book." José's artistry in *Coronado's Friars* bears out Chávez' faith in the El Paso artist. The frontispiece José did for the book is truly memorable. Using the general shape of a triangle, which José finds artistically satisfying, he placed standing figures at the left, kneeling or seated ones in the middle, and on the right a tiny Indian pueblo with smoke arising from it, all stretched across the broad canvas of a Southwestern desert. The vastness of the challenge that faced the *Conquistadores* and the *padres* who came to the region is beautifully symbolized, yet the graphic details are far more than symbolic. They are real, stark and vivid, and only slightly softened, as if by time and distance.

This frontispiece caught the eye of bookdealer Jack E. Reynolds of Van Nuys, California, who asked José to create a similar scene for a book catalog cover. Dr. Joseph Shebel of Salinas, California, asked for another to be drawn for him, and after José had done several more drawings for him, Dr. Shebel invited José and Vicenta out for a private showing of José's art to friends and western art fans — who bought up the entire lot!

Angélico Chávez' *Archives of the Archdiocese of Santa Fe* is enriched by endpapers, maps, and decorations by Cisneros, including a drawing of *La Conquistadora* — Our Lady of the Conquest — a tribute to the statue of the Virgin that survived the Pueblo Revolt in New Mexico in the 1680s.

With such opportunities to illustrate publications with a religious nature, not to omit José's gifts of his talents to regional churches and his own very devoted attendance at St. Joseph's church near his home, it was only natural in 1962 for him to be asked by the Confraternity of Christian Doctrine to illustrate a series of 24 leaflets, *Religión en el Hogar*, for the instruction of Spanish-speaking children in the Catholic home. The folders that enclose the two dozen leaflets have a familiar historic ring, displaying a Spanish *padre* in front of a mission, teaching a group of Indian children of various ages. Each leaflet has its own sketch — a laughing girl, a boy on a see-saw, a family saying grace — that must have helped reach countless young minds at their most impressionable ages.

Back in the 1950s when Texas Attorney General Will Wilson was fighting the battle of the tidelands all the way to the Supreme Court, a different series of the work of José Cisneros appeared in newspapers across the state. It was entitled "The Shape of Texas," as Sue Flanagan recalls. A creative member of Wilson's staff, she worked with José as he developed a group of 12 drawings that brought to life some of the interstate battles over boundaries that made the outline of Texas what it is today. The first dealt with "No Man's Land," the area literally between Texas and Louisiana, where eight oil fields are coveted by tax collectors of both states. Another features a lawyer studying an ancient tree that figured in marking a part of the border of Texas. As always, José's study of history was called upon as well as his talented use of the pen.

Another series of drawings, done to aid Carl Hertzog in an advertising venture, adorned a 1948 set of newspaper advertisements for the State National Bank of El Paso. A natural concept for two such lovers of the history of the area, the weekly series called "Signposts of Early El Paso" gave José opportunity to educate El Pasoans with a wide variety of historical notes about his adopted city: the wooden boot of Kenneth and Filmore's shoe shop, the public notice tree in Pioneer Plaza, the coming of electricity to the pioneer town, and other fascinating details of life from the 19th century were all presented with artistry and accuracy. The series was reissued several years later in a slim booklet celebrating the bank's 75th anniversary

by C. L. SONNICHSEN

The

EL PASO SALT WAR

of 1877

Illustrations by
JOSÉ CISNEROS

Typography by
CARL HERTZOG

A 1961 publication of Texas Western Press, this is an outstanding example of Cisneros/Hertzog dust jackets.

— a booklet that is indeed a treasure for anyone interested in the history of El Paso, or in the talents of José Cisneros.

Dr. Castañeda was right on target when, in a book he gave to José, he described Cisneros as "*enamorado del pasado heroico de la Conquista de América y del más fiel compañero del conquistador, su caballo*" (enamored of the heroic past of the conquest of America and of the most faithful companion of the Conquistador, his horse.) That love of the past, and his fascination with the horse and horsemen, have been at the heart of José's success as an artist.

They say that everyone loves a good tale, a bonnie tune, and a picture worth lingering over. But the ones who really know horses and horsemanship, those who care about accuracy and historical truth, those who want true pictures to linger over — all these really appreciate the skills of José Cisneros.

Carl Hertzog tells the story of a series of pictures José drew that were being published in celebration of the 289th anniversary of the founding of the city of Juárez. José also

The Mexican Eagle in ascendancy over Spanish domination, symbolized by the coat of arms of Castille and Leon, graces the cover of a monograph on that subject by Félix D. Almaráz, Jr., historian at the University of Texas at San Antonio.

wrote the legends — the explanatory material — and he was greatly concerned that the pictures and the words be properly matched. Sure enough, in the rush of putting things together for the press, a pair of captions were mismatched. After it was too late to correct, someone told José not to be too concerned, that not one reader in a thousand would even notice! José replied "That's the one person I'm concerned about." It is his concern for the accuracy expected by one reader in a thousand that has made western historian John M. Carroll call him "my friend, a world famous artist, and a shining star of Texas," in a specially bound copy of *Custer in Texas*, which Carroll chose José to illustrate with eleven drawings. (Joe Grandee also supplied one, and several of Buck Schiwetz' existing drawings were used as well.)

Another who knows José's field, Paul Rossi, former director of the Gilcrease Institute of American Art and History, has called him "beyond any doubt, the leading authority in the country concerning the many varied horsemen of Spanish American history and horsemen of our own Southwest." Others are no less enthusiastic about José's work. Vice President George Bush is a Cisneros collector, and on the occasion of José's sending him a numbered and signed copy of *Riders of the Borderlands*, wrote a letter of appreciation that concluded "We have several of your pictures hanging here in our official residence. We love them all." To which his wife added "We really do!! Warmly, Barbara."

On the flyleaf of a book presented by former Senator Ralph W. Yarbrough appears this accolade:

> For José Cisneros, artist of all the cultures of Texas — Indian, Spanish, French, American, Mexican, Texas, Confederate, and now the new immigrations across the Rio Grande from the south and across Red River from the north, and who can authentically and faithfully capture with colors on paper the spirit of all of them, from Spanish Conquistadores to Indian chiefs to Southern planters. With the esteem of your friend,
>
> *Ralph W. Yarbrough*
> Austin, Texas

A retired cavalryman, General James H. Polk, president of the Board of Trustees of the United States Horse Cavalry Museum, received a portfolio of José's drawings in early 1984, and his response is certainly one of the artist's prizes:

> Dear Mr. Cisneros,
>   Your pen and ink drawings of our Southwestern Horse Soldiers are superb and I shall always treasure them. I didn't realize until I got them home and looked at them carefully that you started with the Conquistador and covered each significant change of uniform and equipment down to our last U.S. Cavalry horse soldier.
>   Also I was charmed by your attention to detail; I couldn't fault it, and the backgrounds are also interesting and add to the visual effect. You are most gifted.
>   Thank you again, and warmest regards.
>
> Most sincerely,
James H. Polk
General, USA Ret.

Such letters and inscriptions from knowledgeable people number in the hundreds in José's collection of memorabilia. José is not a prophet without honor in his own country — far from it: Armando Chávez, old-time associate in *El Ateneo Fronterizo*, encouraged José to design the coat of arms for Ciudad Juárez; it is carved above the door of the Palacio Municipal — and appears on the cover of Chávez' *Historia de Ciudad Juárez, Chihuahua*. Dr. Cleofas Calleros often used José's work in historical or religious publications and projects. El Paso organizations — The El Paso Country Club, The El Paso County Historical Society, and an ecumenical assortment of churches and synagogues, women's clubs and civic groups — have adorned their letterheads and yearbooks and publications, often at little or no cost, with the artistry of José Cisneros. When José was entered into the El Paso County Historical Society Hall of Honor, the certificate presented to him was one he himself had designed, and which had been used previously to honor Carl Hertzog and, later, Tom Lea.

ESCUDO DE ARMAS DE CIUDAD JUAREZ

Encouraged by his old friend Armando B. Chavez of *El Ateneo Fronterizo*, who had become the assistant to the mayor of Juárez, José submitted this prize-winning design for the coat of arms for that city.

But José's stature has brought him honors in many forms and places. He is an honorary Tigua Indian; a Juárez group, *"Pensamiento en acción"* — thought in action — honored him in connection with the publication of Cleofas Calleros' history of Our Lady of Guadalupe in 1959; the City of San Antonio has twice honored him, as "Honorary *Jefe Político* of Bexar County" and as *"Emisario de las musas;"* the League of United Latin American Citizens gave him their Award of Merit; he has received The Daughters of the American Revolution Americanism Medal; and in 1981 the Texas Catholic Historical Society presented José with their highest award, the Reverend Paul J. Foic, CSC Award. In February, 1982, he was presented with the *Gran Paseño* award by UT El Paso President Haskell Monroe, one of the first two such awards, with a certificate José himself had designed. When he was named the fourth recipient of the Dobie-Paisano Fellowship, he was given a six-month residence at the old Dobie ranch near Austin, where he indulged himself by working on his beloved *Riders of the Borderlands.*

First fruits of that fellowship were immediately gathered: an exhibit of his horsemen was presented at the Institute of Texan Cultures in San Antonio, the Humanities Research Center in Austin, at the Palace of the Governors in Santa Fe — as well as Portales, New Mexico; Tucson, Arizona; Mexico City; Los Angeles and Stockton, California; Harlingen, Edinburg, Canyon, and Lubbock, Texas. His horsemen were featured at the opening of The El Paso Cavalry Museum, and have been shown at both the El Paso Museum of Art and the El Paso Centennial Museum. His horsemen have indeed carried his fame far and wide.

Recently my nine-year-old son, exploring José's art studio, asked José: "Are you famous?" With a twinkle in his eye José replied with characteristic modesty, "Your father is trying to make me so." As I tried to set the record straight, I was reminded of the little story "*Un Viaje*" written nearly sixty years ago, and the concluding point that young José had made, namely that the student was the last to admit his own success. The mature José is like that boy still, despite the honors that have come his way. His work has been published by Devin-Adair, Random House, Liveright, Stemmer House, and Alfred A. Knopf. He was named by Western authority Jeff Dykes as one of the *Fifty Great Western Illustrators.* Harold McCracken, former director of the Whitney Gallery of Western Art in Cody, Wyoming, writing of his outstanding book *The American Cowboy,* told José: "The pictures you made for my book are highly cherished among my collection of original Remingtons, Russells, Sharps. . . ." Such accolades surely rank José among the best — yet he is not resting on his laurels.

When McCracken asked for permission to use one of José's horsemen from *Riders of the Border,* the artist hesitated. "It's not quite right," José said. "I'll re-do it for you." On the third try, the result was finally good enough in José's eyes to send to McCracken.

This pattern of striving for perfection, despite all the praise he has earned, suggests that the *viaje* — the artistic journey — of José

Cisneros will continue to unfold as he tries ever harder to become the artist the Lord intended him to be.

It is my belief that the work of José Cisneros will continue to benefit us all. This collection of drawings that cover four centuries of horses and men in the Spanish Borderlands is a significant part of a legacy that he continues to expand — a legacy that will continue to enrich the literature and art of his adopted country.

— John O. West

the artist. . .

and his work. . .

Soldier with Cortés

c. 1519

SPANISH PREDOMINANCE in the Western hemisphere and the expansion of their frontier began with the landing of Captain Hernán Cortés at Veracruz on April 19, 1519. Their continuing thrust northward covered what we now recognize as the Spanish Borderlands.

The contemporary accounts of the conquest of Mexico indicate that the conquerors were a hardy, adventurous and unruly crowd. Cortés' men lacked military experience, carried equipment that was insufficient for the perils of the journey, and were guided primarily by their faith and their ambition.

The appearance and countenance of a horse soldier at the time of the conquest of Mexico was almost medieval. He must have been equipped with odd and outdated pieces of armor, a *bascinet* or a *sallet* for a head covering, a chain mail coat or a cuirass, a sword, dagger or lance and the ever present *adarga*, which was an oval shield inherited from the Moors, made of stiff, heavy leather or rawhide. The round iron shields were called *rodelas*. Sixteen horses and a very limited number of firearms constituted the basis of their offensive power.

Spanish *Conquistador*

c. 1520

Cortes must be considered among the most outstanding leaders of the world. The fact that he embarked upon a conquest of a strange land, with no knowledge of its climate, people, customs, religions or resources, inspires awe and admiration. His abilities and accomplishments were many, and included the establishment, in a new country, of a European culture and language, along with the Christian religion. In time, he also successfully achieved the unification of a Mexican nation. Furthermore, it was Cortés who introduced horsemanship into the region.

The dress of the conquistador includes a helmet of the late 15th century; armor with a heavy cloth skirt, called a *faldar;* a double-handed sword known as a *mandoble;* a foot soldier's halberd which was a very efficient pole arm; and single pointed spurs. Jingling bells were attached to the breast and croup straps of the saddles to impress the natives and create turmoil among them.

Don Hernán Cortés
c. 1526

AN AUTHORITY on the prevailing custom of dress once commented on the capriciousness of fashion and how it has changed through the centuries, either by the whim of a king or a courtesan, or by the discovery of a continent or a silkworm cocoon.

The discovery of a continent gave Spain tremendous influence on sixteenth-century European styles. Spanish apparel was characterized by its elegance, austerity, rigidity and superb decoration and craftsmanship. Gold and silver thread, precious stones, also feathers and ribbons were extensively used in its manufacture and ornamentation.

The discovery of virgin mines, abundance of natural resources, rich and extensive pasturage and cheap labor from the conquered natives resulted in a prosperity without precedent for the new masters of the land. The rider typifies their affluence and ostentation that sometimes surpassed that of their peers at court on the Peninsula.

Don Francisco Vásquez de Coronado
c. 1540

HIGH ON THE LIST of dramatic moments in the history of the Southwest was the expedition of Don Francisco Vásquez de Coronado that took him from the tropical lands of western Mexico to the remote plains of the Texas Panhandle and southern Kansas.

The idea of an exploration of the northern Indian kingdoms developed in the mind of Don Antonio de Mendoza, first viceroy of New Spain, after hearing the stories told by Alvar Núñez Cabeza de Vaca, who previously and fortuitously had traversed the land as a castaway from the ill-fated expedition to Florida in the year 1528.

Mendoza, anxious to please the sovereign and gain honor for himself, hastily secured permission from the crown to organize and finance the enterprise. He commissioned Coronado, at that time the governor of Nueva Galicia, as commander-in-chief of the expedition into the unconquered and unknown region.

It is significant that in their northward thrust, this group of daring adventurers brought with them, along with many types of domestic animals, the first horses to the Southwest.

Spanish Soldier

c. 1550

A MILITARY UNIFORM as a fixed form of dress that was officially prescribed and regulated was not known in the sixteenth century. Troops did not wear similar attire; soldiers were free to choose doublets and breeches of whatever cut and color they liked, and whatever decorative plumes and ribbons they preferred. Civilians could be distinguished from those in the military only by the defensive and offensive weapons worn by the latter. This rider is wearing a cuirass over the fashionable attire of that era and a soft, low-crown hat with narrow brim. The sleeves of the doublet are slashed and puffed as are his soft leather shoes.

Encomendero

c. 1550

IN EUROPE in the fifteenth and early sixteenth century, it was considered proper and legal to consider victims of conquests outside European territory to be barbarians and as such, subject to enslavment. This notion was introduced in the New World by Columbus when he occupied Santo Domingo, and continued to be enforced by his followers on expeditions further inland.

In Mexico, most of the *conquistadores* felt that they deserved a reward for services rendered to the crown and they demanded compensation. Most of the land was divided by Cortés and those who succeeded him into *encomiendas* or *repartimientos*. The *encomendero* or holder of an *encomienda* was entitled to the labor of the Indians on his land. In exchange, he was responsible for the laborers' physical and spiritual welfare. The *encomendero* was usually a soldier or courtier whose services or connections were important enough to earn him the grant.

Fray Bartolomé de las Casas, the first bishop of Chiapas, was an eloquent and untiring defender of the Indians. After making several voyages to Spain, he succeeded in having the *encomiendas* abolished.

Oidor — Spanish Magistrate
Latter half of the XVI Century

DURING THE AFTERMATH of the conquest, Cortés was busy consolidating his possessions in Mexico, when he heard of new discoveries being made in Central America. Not satisfied with what he had already accomplished, he sent Cristóbal de Olid to seize and usurp power from the newcomers there. However Olid rebelled against him and in order to keep him in line, Cortés decided to go to Central America himself. It not only proved to be a disastrous expedition, it also left the government in Mexico in the hands of envious and unscrupulous persons. This created great problems not only for Cortés, but also for the crown.

In the middle of this exasperating anarchy, Charles V instituted the *audiencia*, a tribunal with the power to restore order, and to rule and impart justice. The *audiencia* consisted of five selected judges, one the presiding judge. The establishment of the *audiencia* displaced Cortés as Governor and Captain-General.

The members of the *audiencia* were called *oidores* and when appearing in court they would dress pompously in doctor-at-law robes, with maces and caps styled like those worn during the middle ages.

The Lord Archbishop of Mexico
Mid-XVI Century

In SPAIN, CHURCH AND STATE were intimately related
to each other, with most of the activities revolving and de-
pending on this union. The King was formally addressed as
"His Catholic Majesty," and several of the archbishops became viceroys of New Spain.

Many of the religious festivities, customs and celebrations
were transplanted from the mother country to the newly discovered territories. Sometimes religious ceremonies themselves were accompanied by processions, in addition to the
great public processions that varied according to a particular
diocese or to local established usage and tradition. They were
regulated by special liturgies which formed a separate ritual
that was termed *Procesional*. Palm Sunday, Corpus Christi,
Ascension and Pentecost were appropriate dates for a procession. Certain other circumstances, such as a calamity, the
dedication of a new church, the entry of a new viceroy, or a
patron saint's day also called for such an event.

Usually, when traveling distance between two locales was
great, the Archbishop, attired in the splendor of his ecclesias-
tic robes, would ride on a richly caparisoned mule while be-
stowing blessings and prayers upon the devout multitude.

Spanish Nobleman

c. 1560

THE RENAISSANCE was primarily an artistic movement that originated in Italy and was contemporaneous with the discovery of America. Its foremost aim was to revive the traditions of classical antiquity. It greatly affected and changed the medieval concepts of costume, art, letters and architecture. The movement was promptly accepted by the Mediterranean countries, especially Spain which had strong ties with Italy. Early in the sixteenth century, Spain began to take the lead in fashion as well as in military strength. The enormous riches, derived from the gold and silver mines of Mexico and Peru, transformed her into the most powerful European country. Wealth and political influence provided easy access to the new nobility that was arising in the colonies, and provided those recent aristocrats with ample opportunity to display their affluence.

The Viceroy

THE GREAT DISTANCE that separated Mexico from Spain made it difficult for the court in Madrid to rule the new found lands. After several attempts to consolidate the government, the court decided to institute the viceregal system. This form of government brought about a complete change in public administration. The Viceroy was the sole head of state and as such, represented and exercised royal authority over the colony. That is to say, he acted in place of the king. During the three centuries of Spanish rule, a total of sixty-four viceroys exercised authority over the new territories.

This drawing is a representative portrayal of a viceroy during the period when King Philip II had such influence over fashion. Afflicted with deep religious fervor and a somber disposition, this sovereign introduced into his court the austerity of his convictions and demanded that his subjects use dark colors in their attire. The impact of his dictatorial desires was so far-reaching that scores of years after his death, black remained the predominant color among government officials.

Here the Viceroy wears a ruffled collar known in Spain as a *gorguera*. It is said that at this particular time, the ruffles became so large and unwieldy that an underprop was devised to hold them up. His hat (perhaps a forerunner of our stovepipe hats) was originally named *a la Felipe Segundo*. His richly caparisoned horse and the attire of the herald reflect the wealth of the aristocracy of that period.

El Adelantado Don Juan de Oñate
c. 1598

WHEN PERMISSION was given by the crown to make new conquests of unknown regions, the title of *Adelantado* was often granted to the person in command of the expedition. The title meant that the king recognized that individual as governor of the territory even before it was conquered. Don Juan de Oñate was one of the few to bear that title. Pedro de Alvarado in Guatemala, Francisco de Montejo in Yucatán, and Nuño de Guzmán in Michoacán, shared the same privilege.

The *Adelantado* reached the Rio Grande on April 29, 1598. Although tired and weary after the long journey, the next day he traveled up the river where, after mustering his entire company, he executed, with the pomp and dignity that was customary on such occasions, the *toma de posesión*. This was a legal, elaborate and very formal ceremony, executed upon taking possession of new territory.

From the area around what was later to become El Paso, Oñate proceeded with a band of selected men to secure the obedience of the Indians farther up river before they took fright or organized for war. Answering his summons, the Indian chiefs met at the pueblo that the Spaniards named Santo Domingo, the same Santo Domingo that may be visited today, located north of Albuquerque, New Mexico. It was there that the ceremony took place, the ceremony of accepting Spanish vassalage as well as the Christian faith.

Soldier-Herd Driver with Oñate
c. 1598

T HE SPANIARDS were very punctilious and exacting in their record-keeping. Every item of supplies and equipment in the Oñate expedition was listed, checked and inspected by government officials. The inventory included such listings as "fifty-six Tlaxcala tassels for rosaries" and "twenty whistles of Texcoco clay." However, in some instances, it was more difficult to keep an accounting, especially with the livestock. In his personal report to the viceroy, the Count of Monterrey, Oñate mentioned this problem when he wrote: "Still another difficulty, no less imposing than the ones I have mentioned, is the conservation of the horses and mules, of which there are now more than twelve hundred, not counting more than three hundred horses and mules which have disappeared from the camp in the last thirty days."

With one hundred and thirty families, eighty-three wagons and more than seven thousand animals that included slow-moving sheep and hogs, keeping track of all aspects of the expedition was indeed a difficult task. The soldiers had the dual role of maintaining the safety of the caravan as well as taking turns at herding the animals.

Physician of New Spain
Early XVII Century

I<small>N</small> <small>HIS</small> *History of Medicine in Mexico*, Francisco Flores states that "before the coming of the Spaniards, Indian medicine was very advanced. Aztec physicians knew and could distinguish most illnesses of the human body. They could extract tumors, do amputations, cure fractures, wounds and ulcers." When Philip II sent his learned doctor Francisco Hernández to study the medicinal plants of New Spain, the natives were able to identify for him more than 1200 different species with their respective Mexican names and their uses in medicine. They used some plants like *peyote*, and certain mushrooms and *ololiuhqui* as anesthetics.

The medical knowledge acquired from the Aztec healers by both the Spanish physicians and the missionaries was put to good use in the several hospitals established right after the conquest. The Hospital de Jesús in Mexico City was the first one on the American continent. It was founded in 1523 by Cortés at his own expense, and without interruption it continued to be — and still is — in service. The one that followed was named Hospital Real de San José de los Naturales. It was founded by Fray Pedro de Gante in 1531 to serve the Indians exclusively.

Spanish *Conquistador*
Early XVII Century

WITH THE CONQUEST CONSOLIDATED, Cortés made an effort to establish some consistency in the martial readiness of the new overlords of Mexico. In one of his ordinances in March, 1524, he introduced obligatory service under arms for all Spanish colonists, settlers and immigrants of the conquered region. All of them were required to present themselves every four months at muster, equipped with sets of arms in proportion to the value of their estates. The minimum equipment each of the militiamen had to carry was a helmet, shield, lance, sword and dagger. Landlords with more than 500 Indian servants and laborers were each required to have a horse with harness and saddle. Noncompliance could result in heavy fines to be paid in gold. Continuing failure to comply meant that the recalcitrant's labor force could be taken away. This ordinance continued in force throughout the sixteenth century. From this it can be assumed that many later *conquistadores* had previously been trained as militiamen.

Interest in things military was kept alive by the arrival every six months of Spanish fleets in Mexican waters. On those ships came detachments of the royal army of Spain which landed at the ports for the special purpose of instructing the citizens in the handling of arms, military tactics and exercises. At the conclusion of the training, the army detachment would return to Spain with the next outgoing fleet, to be replaced by a new detachment brought in by the next incoming fleet.

New Mexico *Encomendero*
Early XVII Century

PAUL HORGAN, in his book *Great River*, gives a very satisfactory description of the *encomienda* system. He calls it a "provision of guardianships by which each Spanish landholder had 'commended' to him the Indians who lived on his land. He was to be responsible to them, in their spiritual and physical welfare. In return, their work was owed to him and their defense of the land." Thirty-five *encomiendas* were apparently made in the seventeenth century, mostly for defensive purposes, since the royal government could not defend the region effectively without them, and since there was no presidio in New Mexico until after the Pueblo Revolt. *Encomenderos* were permitted to collect tributes from the Indians, in the form of labor, grain crops or cotton cloth. The *encomenderos* were also obliged to participate, with their arms, horses and Indian subjects, in the defense of the realm from the marauding Apaches.

The *encomendero* in seventeenth-century New Mexico was also, for the reasons stated above, Captain of Militia. The *encomiendas* were evidently abolished early in the eighteenth century, since it was during that time that Governor de Vargas' request for an *encomienda*, in return for his services to the crown, was denied.

Spanish Soldier in Trouble
Early XVII Century

When the spaniards brought their horses to the New World, the Indians were terrified of the huge creatures that they had never seen before. But once that initial terror had subsided, they looked upon the animals with envy and an intense desire to possess them. The Spainards, however, guarded their herds, and wherever they pushed their conquests, they forbade Indians to own horses.

In the northern reaches of New Spain, in 1680, the Indians rebelled against the Iberian intruders, drove them out of Santa Fe and its environs, and forced them to leave most of their stock behind. Not for twelve years did the conquerors return, and in those years their horses ran wild. The Indians began to capture them, raise them, and even trade the animals eastward.

By the 1700s practically all the tribes in the buffalo country of the Great Plains had obtained horses and had learned to ride. With no rules to follow "they learned to ride by riding, just as their horses learned to travel by traveling," wrote J. Frank Dobie. The newly acquired horse gave the Indian strong feelings of well-being never experienced by him before; it also gave him great mobility, pride, self-confidence, and a taste for revenge.

From the moment the Indian was raised from his earthbound condition by the acquisition of the horse, the conquerors realized with dismay that in the future they would have to face their foes in battle on almost equal terms.

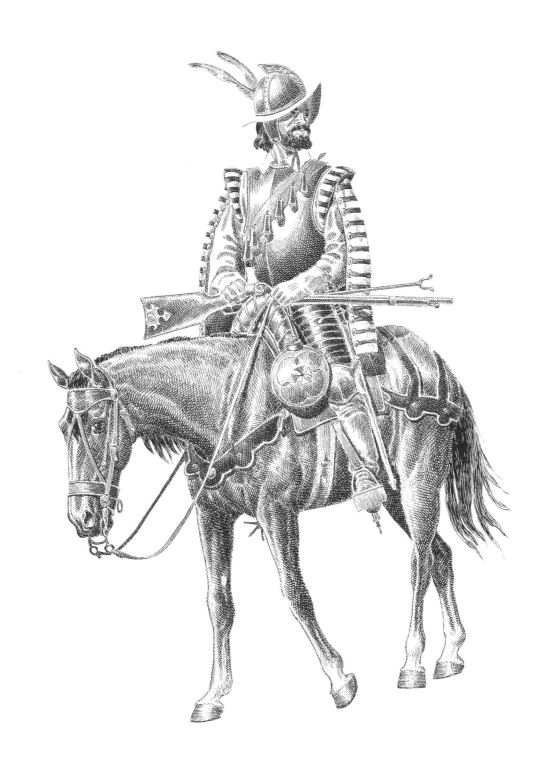

Spanish Explorer
Late XVI Century

SPAIN WAS THE FIRST European colonizing power to come to the New World, and the process was carried out by a comparatively small number of adventurers. The achievement of these few men — officers, soldiers and friars, who carved out an empire — is without parallel in world history. The area in which this dream of the *conquistadores* was achieved challenges the imagination: a confused group of nations with different names, with hundreds of languages and dialects and different gods, scattered over the entire continent. Yet the miracle was that the Spanish Empire of the Americas, in spite of all obstacles, lasted for three centuries.

Hispanic influence in western North America had its roots in sixteenth-century exploration by men in armor such as Francisco Vásquez de Coronado and the great Portuguese sailor Juan Rodríguez Cabrillo, who reconnoitered the region by land and by sea in a futile search for wealthy kingdoms to match those found in Mexico and Peru.

It is truly amazing that by the end of the sixteenth century the Spanish explorers had criss-crossed most of the American continent, they had discovered most of the mining fields, and they had left their *pasó por aquí* inscriptions in the most unsuspected and remote places.

Such men as Francisco de Ibarra, Francisco de Urdiñola, Antonio de Espejo, Juan de Oñate, and Gaspar Castaño de Sosa greatly increased the geographical knowledge of Mexico in the sixteenth century.

Spanish Noblewoman
Early XVII Century

DURING THE SPANISH COLONIAL PERIOD, life for the women was restricted almost exclusively to the home. In a traditionalist, deeply religious environment, with a code of ethics that favored the male, the woman's activities and personal freedom were greatly curtailed. It was the father, husband, or brother who dictated and imposed the rules of conduct and behavior. The affairs of government, trade and professions were forbidden territories for females. This is why so very few women ever achieved prominence during the viceregal period. One of the exceptions was Sor Juana Inés de la Cruz, a nun who is considered to have been the greatest poetess Mexico has ever produced.

However for most of them in those bygone days, particularly the women of nobility, the primary responsibilities were to take care of the family and servants, follow the fashion trends, assist in giving parties, visit with friends and above all, to attend religious festivities. Other pastimes included picnics, promenading and horseback riding.

Juego de Cañas
c. 1650

ONLY *a la jineta* riding was practical for many of the favorite horseback sports, such as *juego de cañas* which translates literally as caneplay. This was an ancient Arab game that was brought to Spain by the Moslem conquerors. It was of course played on horseback and it simulated a battle, with the canesticks taking the place of javelins. The players, in formation and at full speed, threw the sticks at one another and the purpose of the game was to catch them without being hit. In their tournaments, extra long leather shields were used, each painted with the caballero's personal armorial emblem.

Una de las bravas
mujeres españolas

IN THE NUMEROUS REPORTS concerning the Spanish expeditions which reached the territory that later became the American Southwest, credit for those enterprises is usually given to the fearless, intrepid, daring and courageous soldiers and adventurers who engaged in the conquest. Seldom if ever are women mentioned, yet from the beginning, several women were members of some of those expeditions. For example, the muster dated 1540, under the leadership of Francisco Vásquez de Coronado, lists "Francisca de Hozes, wife of the shoemaker; Maria Maldonado, who became the army's nurse; and the native wife of Lope Caballero, all made the long trip to Cíbola." In 1582 Don Antonio de Espejo, accompanied by fifteen soldiers and a group of servants, came to Paso del Norte for the purpose of rescuing Fray Agustín Rodríguez and his companions. Among the soldiers was one Miguel Sánchez Valenciano who brought his wife Casilda de Amaya and his sons Miguel, Lázaro, Pedro and Juan. It is said that Pedro was three-and-a-half years old, and Juan was a twenty-month-old baby.

In 1590 an unauthorized expedition, headed by Gaspar Castaño de Sosa, came from New Almadén, Coahuila, and reached Pecos and the Pueblo of Santo Domingo, New Mexico. Several families came with the expedition. Later, many brave women arrived with Oñate's group and settled in that same region which now includes Santa Fe and the surrounding area.

Spanish Nobleman

c. 1650

IN ORDER to understand the role that the titled nobility played in the day-to-day life of New Spain, one has to delve into the intricacies of history. In a rare study of the Spanish Military Orders in Mexico, Leopoldo Martínez Cosío obtained some interesting facts about their origin, activities, and their influence in government, civil and religious life.

The military Orders of Santiago, Calatrava and Alcántara were founded in Spain at the close of the twelfth century, and were based on the rules and regulations of the Knights Templar of Jerusalem. Their purpose was to resist and fight the Moslems that had occupied most of Spain. They came into existance as military-religious institutions to defend Christianity and help the King. They were ruled by a Grand Master, elected by all knights in the Order. The candidates for knighthood were chosen from the nobility and were given great power and influence in governmental affairs.

Along with many other institutions, Spain also brought to America her military orders. According to the study by Martínez Cosío, those who received the habit and the title of the Order of Santiago during the Colonial period in Mexico numbered four hundred and twenty-six. One hundred and twenty-one were in the Calatrava, sixty-six in the Alcántara, six in the Montesa (which was later added), with the remaining eleven in the Order of Malta. Several governors of New Mexico and Nueva Viscaya as well as Presidio Inspectors, high-ranking military officers and prominent citizens of the various provinces boasted titles from one of the various orders.

Spanish Pioneer Woman
c. 1650

ONLY FAITH AND DETERMINATION sustained the brave Spanish women who participated in those early northward expeditions. After undergoing the perils and hardships of the difficult journey, and separated from family and friends, they were then left to their own resources to begin a new life in a strange wilderness. The livelihood of husband, wife and family depended on a joint effort of tilling and planting, raising livestock and other domestic animals.

Typical of the courageous and determined Spanish pioneer is this lady, seated sideways on an *aparejo* or pack-saddle, and holding an infant on her lap. A few household belongings dangle from the saddle, and a simple rope tied in a hackamore knot serves as a bridle.

True to her beliefs and her convictions of loyalty and devotion to her sovereign, the Spanish pioneer woman made the journey to a strange land in order to fulfill his wishes and to help extend and populate his borderlands.

Caballero en Plaza
Late XVII Century

THE TERM *caballero en plaza* is still used in Spain. It is applied to the nonprofessional bullfighter on horseback who goes into the ring, armed with a *rejón*, which is a wooden pole with a barb at one end. This is used to taunt and punish the bull. In this manner the bullfighter displays his horsemanship and skill at royal or charitable festivities. He is a direct descendent of those noble and beautifully attired Spanish cavaliers of the sixteenth and seventeenth centuries who appeared in the arena as *rejoneadores*. It is claimed that one of the first of these gentlemen was King Sebastian of Portugal, grandson of Charles V.

The entertainment and pastimes, inherited from the Romans and the Moors, and brought by the Spaniards to the new lands, included bullfighting. The first formal *corrida* took place in Mexico City on June 24, 1526. In those days the more daring feats in bullfighting were executed on horseback, and the performers were members of the nobility. Very often the Viceroy himself was the star of the show, claiming the center of attention as a true *caballero en plaza*.

Through the years, bullfighting changed and evolved into a profession, where the performers were on foot instead of astride horses, and the position of the *caballero en plaza* was relegated to the honorary and ceremonial role of *alguacil*, with the rider attired in black and heading the procession that takes place before the *corrida*.

The present-day saddle only partly resembles those used by the Portuguese *rejoneadores* during the eighteenth century.

Hidalgo

c. 1670

Whichever term is used, *Hijo de algo, Hijodalgo,* or *Hidalgo,* it means a person on the lowest step of the ladder of nobility. In Spain, the importance given to noble lineage far exceeded that of other countries. Spanish traditionalist society was conditioned to accept the artificial situation of an unwritten code of honour that forbade *hidalgos* to become tradesmen. Thanks to their noble birth, or *hidalguía* they could claim the right to live in unproductive leisure as parasites of the court and drones in their families. Also claiming immunity from work and demanding special privileges and concessions were those who gloried in the title of "Don," a title that was frequently self-acquired.

Another peculiar abberation was the cult of *limpieza de sangre,* or purity of blood, which was of fundamental importance in the social, religious and political history of Spain. The requirements for any pretendants to any public office in Church and State demanded that they have no Jewish or Moorish blood in their veins. These ideas accompanied those who settled in the Colonies where, for lack of other matters to discuss, our Spanish ancestors spent much time and effort in attempting to convince others of the purity of their blood.

Don Diego de Vargas
Reconqueror of New Mexico
c. 1692

MANY HISTORIANS have given full accounts of the adventures and deeds of the reconqueror of New Mexico, the length of whose name — Don Diego José de Vargas Zapata Luján Ponce de León y Contreras — indicates at least a touch of conceit.

Paul Horgan, in his book, *Conquistadors in North American History*, describes him as a magnificent semblance of a man. This impression is no doubt based on the portrait done of Don Diego de Vargas in Madrid and which is kept in the chapel of San Isidro in the Pretil de Santiesteban.

"A fine drawn and elegant aristocrat, tall, dark and thin, he wore his black hair parted in the middle and swept to his shoulders on either side of his long, oval face," Horgan says. "His complexion was smooth in a pale olive color, and his eyes, under level, dark brows, had a calm power of observation and command. He wore his mustaches trimmed in a narrow line and his beard was a mere pencil line on his strong chin. His nose was long and straight and his mouth in repose was level and neither great-lipped nor small.

"In the heavy velvets of court dress," Horgan continues, "edged with fur and picked out with gold bullion lace, and tasselled at the knees of his short breeches, and bloused in ballooning fine linen, and bearing a velvet hat circled in plumes, he presented a figure of grave elegance; and in the leather thigh boots, armor, and rain-shedding broadcloth cloak of the mounted officer in the field, he carried an air of just and incontrovertible command."

Father Eusebio Francisco Kino

c. 1700

FATHER EUSEBIO FRANCISCO KINO deserves a very special place among the explorers and settlers of the West. In recognition of his merit, the State of Arizona declared him an outstanding son, and in Washington, D.C., a statue of him was placed in the National Statuary Hall. Father Kino was a missionary, a man of science and letters, geographer, explorer, builder, and stockman. In addition, he was an extraordinary horseman.

He holds the honor or establishing the first Spanish settlements in the *Pimería Alta*, as Arizona was then called. In addition to being the founder of many missions, he also established livestock breeding centers from which came thousands of animals. Father Kino's accomplishments just as a ranchman would stamp him as an unusual businessman. One example of his business acumen is the operation at the Mission San Xavier del Bac (near Tucson, Arizona) which he started with seven hundred head of cattle from the herds of Mission Dolores that he had previously established. At Mission San Xavier del Bac, he transformed unruly nomadic Indians into self-supporting people. He had great fascination for all types of domestic animals and was particularly proud of the two huge sheepskins that covered his bed, because the hides were from rams in his own corrals.

A remarkable and practical frontiersman, Father Kino carried the cross in one hand and the branding iron in the other.

Spanish Officer
Early XVIII Century

THE EIGHTEENTH CENTURY brought considerable changes into the colony of New Spain. In the matter of military attire, it witnessed, by way of Spain, the introduction of Dutch or Walloon uniforms brought by Flemish troops sent by the crown to revitalize her army. These uniforms, in turn, imitated the French style which was becoming predominant throughout Europe.

The wide brimmed hat, sometimes upturned on one side, replaced the cap or helmet. The coat was tight-fitting above the waist, knee length and flaring out over the hips. It buttoned down the front and had long, full cuffs turned back and fastened with buttons to show the coat lining — thus distinguishing one regiment from another — which was the origin of regimental facings. Two large pockets were set low on the front of the skirts. Under the coat went a thigh-length waistcoat. The legs were clad in loose breeches with ruffles at the knees. Hair was worn long and loose.

Two distinctive features in the Spanish military attire of this period was the red sash, worn by officers across the corselet, and the Burgundy or Saint Andrew's Cross, displayed on banners or standards instead of the traditional royal coat of arms of Castile and León.

El Visitador Don Pedro de Rivera
c. 1726

THE COLORFUL MILITARY LIFE in the early Spanish frontier presidios, then located in today's American West and Southwest, is still only superficially known. The Spanish colonial administration was frequently out of touch with its distant presidios, for reports from the frontier were about as infrequent as the reports from the capital to the forts. In 1724, in a report to his King, the Marquis de Casa Fuerte reported that "the interior presidios of his kingdom existed without regulations or orders." He then drew up a list of rules that would apply to all such outposts.

In order to maintain a thin line of communication between the scattered forts so that a check could be made on how those rules were being followed, and how the King's soldiers were discharging their duties, a new commision was created. It was called *Visitador* (Presidio Inspector) and was usually given to an army officer of field grade who was wise in the ways of the frontier. The job of a *Visitador* was a long-range, arduous, exciting and vital one.

Brigadier Don Pedro de Rivera was commissioned *Visitador* because of his lengthy frontier experience. His long journey of inspection lasted for almost four years, and ranged throughout all the far-flung regions where the presidios were located. He reached Paso del Norte on May 17, 1726.

Spanish-Mexican *Hacendado*

LAND GRANTS that were distributed by the Crown soon after the Conquest became the foundation of the big Mexican haciendas thereafter. This state of things gradually gave way to a peculiar rural society where the *hacendado*, the landowner, began to act as a feudal lord, thus creating a system that would survive until the revolution against the regime of President Díaz in 1910. The *hacendado* was the master and self-appointed authority of his isolated community. His servants were dependent on him for shelter, food, clothing and entertainment in exchange for their labor and freedom. He was even responsible for their religious instruction and rudimentary schooling. The big haciendas were usually self-sufficient with warehouses, workshops and private chapels.

More than any others, the *hacendados* were responsible for the development and evolution of the Mexican riding costume. According to the necessities imposed by the rural environment, they gradually created, adapted or changed their attire, until finally, through the years, it became the country's national costume.

A beautiful copper-plate engraving from the middle of the eighteenth century, in the National Library of Mexico, shows the execution of a criminal in front of the viceregal palace. Among the crowd there are three *rancheros* lavishly attired in the colorful costumes of the period. Another source of information and perhaps the most important pictorial document of the eighteenth century is a painting in the National Museum of History in Chapultepec showing the Plaza Mayor in Mexico City. Characters of all sorts are represented there, from the viceroy on down the social scale to street vendors and beggars. Almost in the foreground, wrapped in their gorgeous *mangas*, (mantles), and with cross stirrups on their saddles, are two dashing *rancheros*.

Baja California Spanish Soldier

c. 1750

A STRANGE, UNPLEASANT INCIDENT that occurred more than two hundred years ago was to provide us with the knowledge of the type of uniforms worn by the Spanish soldiers in the middle of the eighteenth century when they were in Lower California. Don Gaspár de Portolá was appointed governor of the province at San José del Cabo on November 30, 1767. In traveling to his new post, he carried the order of expulsion of the Jesuits from that province, as decreed by King Carlos III. The first in the group of Jesuits to learn of this order was Father Ignacio Tirsch, a Bohemian-born priest in charge of Misión de Santiago. When the order of expulsion was implemented, Father Tirsch took with him a portfolio of watercolors that he had done at the mission, depicting birds, plants, building, settlers and soldiers. The portfolio survived all the perils of a long journey to different parts of Europe and finally turned up, after more than two hundred years, at the State Library in the University of Prague. From a color reproduction in the original portfolio, we have fashioned a likeness of one of those soldiers, as he appeared to Father Tirsch. The original color reproduction was located by Glen Dawson, a bookdealer from Los Angeles, who published it in book form with the title *The Drawings of Ignacio Tirsch*, with narrative by Doyce B. Nunis, Jr. Our drawing is based on one of the pictures, done by Father Tirsch, of the Lower California Spanish soldiers.

Northern Mexico *Ganadero*

c. 1750

PIERRE MARIE FRANCOIS DE PAGES was a career officer in the French Navy who inexplicably jumped ship in Santo Domingo on June 30, 1767, then journeyed around the world for the next four years. The first leg of his travels took him to New Orleans, then through Texas to Mexico. In de Pagès' narratives of his wanderings, there is a portion of his observations about Texas that concern its horsemen.

"His heels are usually armed with a pair of enormous spurs about five or six inches in length," he says. "Two little leathern boxes placed before the saddle serve to hold provisions for his march. His saddle-leathers neatly dressed, and stamped with various ornamental designs, are garnished round the edges with trinkets of steel which, like as many little bells, are kept perpetually ringing by the motion of his horse. The rider rests his feet in a couple of stirrups at least fifty pounds of weight, which are composed of four 'massy' bars of iron arranged in the form of a cross. To keep the horseman steady in his seat and to constrain his limbs to that position which is deemed most graceful among the Spaniards, are the chief purpose of those ponderous stirrups. The bits of their bridles are extremely adapted to their purpose.

"In fact," de Pagès continues, "the half-savage Spaniard, with all this singular extravagance, is an excellent rider, and when completely equipped and mounted, never failed to revive in my mind all the ideas of ancient chivalry. . ."

Don José de Escandón —
Colonizer of the Lower Rio Grande
1747-1755

During the eighteenth century, perhaps the most successful colonizer of the borderlands was Don José de Escandón, in his occupation of Nuevo Santander in the region between the Pánuco River and the Lower Rio Grande lands. According to his contemporaries, Escandón was a man of integrity, energy, intelligence and ambition. He was born in Soto la Marina, in the province of Santander, Spain. He arrived in Mexico when he was 16 years old, and resided in Yucatan before making his home in Querétaro, where he became *Corregidor*, or mayor of the city. Very active in the army, he led several campaigns against the rebel Chichimeca Indians and achieved the pacification of the Sierra Gorda region at his own expense.

The threat of the French and the British on the Gulf Coast induced the royal authorities to settle that isolated region. Escandón, who had been trying to persuade the viceroy to do just that, was appointed governor and lieutenant general of the colonizing expedition. So successful was he in the enterprise that in only seven years he established twenty-three self-sufficient civil settlements along the Bajo Rio Grande. Although the settlers engaged in various activities, ranching remained the dominant occupation. Their prosperity surpassed that of the neighboring province of Texas.

In recognition of his services to the crown, King Fernando VI rewarded Escandón with the title of Conde de Sierra Gorda and later on with the robes of the prestigious military Order of Santiago.

Northern Mexico Militiaman

c. 1750

THE VAST EXTENSION of Spanish colonies in America, their distance from the metropolis, the relative peace which the colonies enjoyed up to the Wars of Independence, and the military obligations that occupied Spain to her utmost capacity in Europe, were the reasons why the military force in her New World possessions was largely constituted by native contingents in the form of various Trained and Urban Militias (*Milicias Disciplinadas y Urbanas*).

When the need arose to expand colonial armed forces, it became unavoidable to accept enlistment of colored men, but they were separated into racial units. Companies and battalions were raised of white, halfbreed, and Negro elements — *blancos, pardos y morenos*. Toward the end of the eighteenth century the sight of colored militiamen who were uniformed, armed, and many displaying officers' insignia, aroused uneasiness among white Spaniards. Objections and protests were filed with royal authorities claiming that "the halfbreed and Negro militias only serve to fan their vanity; their officers, adorned with uniforms, epaulets and swords, soon aim their thoughts at higher objectives; they disdain cultivating their fields, and abandon agriculture to the labor of whites or of Negro slaves. Sad days will come upon us when Spain finds herself served by mulattoes and Negroes whose suspicious loyalty may cause violent commotions."

The Volunteer Militia of the "back country," that is, northern Mexico, usually dressed in jackets, breeches and leggings of buckskin, with a blue or red *manga*, (mantle), some armed with lances that were fitted with crescent-shaped points, known as *desjarretaderas*.

El Señor Alcalde de Paso del Norte
c. 1760

T HE ORIGINAL MANUSCRIPT of the *Idea compendiosa del Reyno de Nueva España* lies in the Biblioteca Nacional de Madrid. The author of the *Idea*, Pedro Alonso O'Crouley y O'Donnell, was born in Spain, of Irish parents. He made several trips to Mexico between 1764 and 1774 during which he gathered most of the material and information for his manuscript. Seán Galvin of Loughlinstown House, County Dublin, translated it into English and published it for the first time. In the original there were several watercolors reproduced, depicting common characters of the period. We chose one of those to recreate our *Alcalde*, and also present a portion of his description of the Presidio of Paso del Norte, which reads:

"This presidio is situated at 30 degrees north latitude. There is a large population of Spaniards and mestizos because it is on the border of New Mexico where fairs are held, bargains are struck, horses traded, and horsehides, cured sheepskins, buffalo robes and the like, are bought and sold. It is also here that captives who have been ransomed from the heathen tribes are sheltered and instructed in the mysteries of the Faith.

"There is a garrison of eighty soldiers, the spiritual care of which is entrusted to the Mission of Guadalupe, half a league away. Towards the east there is a broad valley with bay trees where wheat, maize, beans, and all manner of garden crops are raised, and there are many vineyards, which yield grapes superior to those of Parras. The abundant water supply from the Rio Grande increases the natural fertility of the land and reduces dependence on rainfall."

Vaquero del Bajo Río Grande

c. 1770

WITH THE COLONIZATION of Nuevo Santander, José de Escandón created the greatest ranching conglomerate on the northern frontier of New Spain. Under his powerful leadership, Reynosa, Camargo, Revilla, Mier, Jiménez, Laredo, and Dolores very rapidly became flourishing livestock-raising communities in the Lower Rio Grande region.

Escandón had carefully recruited his settlers from experienced ranchers and frontiersmen of the pastoral regions of the provinces of Querétaro and San Luis Potosí. He gathered nearly four thousand people who marched northward, driving great herds of cattle, horses, mules, goats and sheep. Included in this crowd was a group known as *soldados pobladores*, or soldier-settlers who agreed to join the expedition, fully armed and equipped at their own expense, on the condition that they could lay claim to choice grazing lands.

The contemporary *Kineños*, or cowboys of the King Ranch, can rightfully trace their ancestry to those daring *vaqueros* who were brought by Escandón, generations ago, to the rich and fertile lands of the Bajo Rio Grande.

Lanceros de Veracruz
Gulf Coast Lancer
c. 1770

W HILE THE "CUERA" DRAGOONS were operating along the northern line of presidios that stretched across our present Southwest from the Pacific to the Gulf of Mexico, another group of soldiers, just as colorful and picturesque, guarded the eastern approaches to New Spain. Known officially as *Lanceros de Vera Cruz*, they operated on the coast from Veracruz to what is now Brownsville, Texas.

Their uniforms consisted of tight-fitting buckskin jackets with puffed and slashed sleeves, reminiscent of the garments of the late sixteenth century and giving them an anachronistic appearance. A wide and beautifully embossed bandolier served as both pistol and sword holder. The sword looked almost like a machete or sugar cane cutting knife, and was known as an *espada ancha*, or broadsword. The saddle was of the *jineta* type, heavily padded and fitted with cross stirrups, the use of which has puzzled many Mexican historians. The rider is wearing a native regional straw hat suitable for the tropical climate.

This rendition is based on a contemporary watercolor found and shared by the late Joseph Hefter, internationally known military historian, artist and translator, and a friend of the author.

California *Cuera* Dragoon
c. 1775

IN 1769, UPPER CALIFORNIA was threatened with a Russian occupation. By this time, Spaniards occupied the Western Hemisphere all the way from Chile to Southern Arizona. A thin line of mission settlements extended two thirds of the way up the long peninsula of Lower California. Here the Spanish advance had come nearly to a standstill. King Carlos III decided that, in order to protect the threatened territory, New California should be settled. The plan provided for Franciscan friars to convert and civilize the Indians, and for soldiers to guard the country and protect the missionaries. Governor Gaspár de Portolá and Father Junípero Serra were the mainstays of the expedition. With them came the first *Cuera* Dragoons to that region. They were transplanted from Lower California, where they had been stationed for several years, to what is now the State of California. A singular and picturesque feature of their uniforms was the leather, buckskin, or sometimes rawhide coat, from which they derived their nickname, *cuera.*

José Cardero, an artist who was a member of the Alejandro Malaspina expedition to Alaska, made several drawings of presidio settlers, including the soldiers, on his visit to Monterey, California in 1791.

Don Hugo Oconór

c. 1775

Britain's religious persecution of Ireland during the sixteenth century caused many of the Irish citizens to immigrate to Spain. Some of those Irish immigrants were recruited into the Spanish army and were sent to New Spain where a number of them played important roles in Southwestern history. One of them was red-headed Hugh O'Connor, who subsequently hispanized his name to Hugo Oconór.

Upon Oconór's arrival in Veracruz he continued his successful army career and eventually was sent to the northern frontier. He succeeded Don Bernardo de Gálvez (later a viceroy of New Spain) as commandant inspector of the frontier posts. Oconór established his headquarters in the little town of San Fernando del Carrizal, located some fifty miles south of Juárez, Mexico, where he was stationed for six years. From his base at Carrizal, he traveled the desert in all directions to visit almost every town on the Spanish frontier. On one of his inspection tours to Arizona, he established on August 20, 1775, the Royal Presidio of San Augustín de Tucsón, known today as Tucson, Arizona. At one time he was governor of Texas and it was then that the Indians nicknamed him "El Capitán Colorado," or Red Captain.

After more than 15,000 miles on horseback throughout the borderlands, the illustrious and courageous frontiersman, Don Hugo Oconór, Knight of the Order of Calatrava, Inspector General of the Internal Provinces of New Spain, Captain General of the Province of Yucatán, died in the City of Mérida on the 8th day of March of the year 1779.

Franciscan Missionary
XVIII Century

THE PRESENCE OF SPAIN in the Southwest was enhanced by the strong support and assistance of the Franciscans. They marked their paths with institutions, monuments and customs that have survived through the centuries. In their journeys they followed Estéban the Moor and Francisco Vásquez de Coronado; they were with Antonio de Espejo and with the Adelantado Don Juan de Oñate. They traversed the land with the soldiers and without them. In their burning zeal to conquer souls, their efforts sometimes culminated in martyrdom.

No group of men had more influence in the founding of the pivotal cities in the Spanish period than the members of the Order of Friars Minor. San Francisco, San Diego, San Antonio, Los Angeles, Guadalupe del Paso del Norte, Ciudad de la Santa Fé de Nuestro Padre San Francisco — all attest and proclaim with their sonorous Spanish names the Franciscan heritage of their origin.

Junípero Serra, Agustín Rodríguez, Antonio Margil de Jesús, Alonso de Benavides, and García de San Francisco are a few of the names in the long and illustrious roster of great *poverellos*, benefactors of the Southwest.

Although in their mission establishments they were surrounded by livestock and all kinds of domestic animals, the statutes of their order and their religious triple vows of poverty, chastity and obedience prevented them from riding horses, except on very extraordinary circumstances.

Arizona Presidial Soldier

c. 1780

THE PRESIDIO OF SAN AGUSTIN DE TUCSON
was established in 1775 by Colonel Hugo Oconór,
Commandant Inspector of all the frontier provinces.
Located in hostile Indian country, the fortified
outpost's function was to assure Spanish occupation
and retention of that vast region of Arizona. It was also
to play an important part in the development of that
area.

In 1785, the Tucson presidio did not yet have a perimeter wall or a gate, according to research conducted by the late Prof. Max L. Moorhead of the University of Oklahoma's Department of History. The pali-
sade, guardhouse, storeroom, cellar and chapel had all
been built at the personal expense of the commandant,
Lt. Colonel Pedro de Allande. The commandant then
adorned the battlements of the partial wall with the
heads of several slain Apaches.

When the presidio was finally completed in 1787, its
adobe brick perimeter wall was two feet thick, 12 feet
high, and it surrounded a 750-square-foot plaza. At di-
agonally opposite corners were lookout towers, and
within the compound a firing platform stretched across
the roofs of the stable, shop and storeroom. Living
quarters for the soldiers and their families were located
along the interior side of the walls, while the more pre-
tentious quarters of the Commandant were in the center of the plaza.

After 1776 the presidio and pueblo of San Agustín de
Tucsón became the major Spanish community in
Pimería Alta, and was manned by *cuera*, or leather-
jacket soldiers.

Captain Don Juan Bautista de Anza

c. 1775

JUAN BAUTISTA DE ANZA, born at the Royal Presidio of Fronteras, Sonora, was a third-generation frontiersman. His grandfather and father before him had served in Sonora. While stationed at Tubac, Arizona, Captain de Anza was chosen to establish much-needed communications with the new settlement in Upper California. With twenty soldiers and sixty head of cattle, he completed the arduous journey to Mission San Gabriel. Beside him rode that intrepid missionary-explorer, Fray Francisco Garcés. When that assignment was completed, de Anza traveled to Mexico City to report to the viceroy, who was very pleased with his accomplishments. Viceroy Bucareli then appointed him to lead a colony to California, using the road that de Anza had opened. Captain de Anza and the colony reached San Francisco Bay where he established a new presidio — one that was to eventually become a prosperous city.

Juan Bautista de Anza's qualities as a leader, pathfinder and colonizer earned him the governorship of New Mexico where he continued his campaigns against the Apaches and Comanches. He also explored new routes of travel that would connect the isolated outposts on the northern frontier.

After 36 years in the service of the crown, he returned to the land of his childhood in Sonora, where he died in 1778. He was buried beneath the wooden floor of the old Jesuit Church of Nuestra Señora de la Asunción in Arizpe, the colonial capital of Sonora.

Mexican Bullfighter on Horseback

c. 1790

IT IS CLAIMED that the Romans introduced a primitive form of bullfighting into Spain some 2000 years ago. Through the years it steadily gained in popularity and even attracted some of the nobility to take part in it. Some of the monarchs, such as Isabella the Catholic of Spain, and in Mexico, the Archbishop-Viceroy Don Juan de Palafox y Mendoza, opposed bullfighting and tried to suppress it, however they were unsuccessful in their attempts.

For the most part, the Spanish sovereigns were not only enthusiastic spectators, but also active participants. Charles V killed one bull at the Plaza of Valladolid, and Philip IV had an active role, on various occasions, in fighting the brave bulls.

Until the middle of the eighteenth century, the *corridas* were held in enclosed plazas of principal cities such as Madrid, and Salamanca. Such cities as these were designed with various closed spaces that could easily be transformed into stadiums. Later on, special bullrings were constructed in both Spain and Mexico. In 1788 the first formal bullring was constructed in Mexico City and named Real Plaza de Toros de San Pablo.

The bullfighter shown here was modeled after an 18th-century painting that is in the possession of Señor Pedro Aspe of Mexico City. In this drawing, the gentleman is wearing a short *manga*, or mantle, breeches split at the knee, and specialy designed, roll-down boots. The saddle is of the type known as *silla de rúa*, with rump housing and heavy cross stirrups.

New Mexico Presidial Soldier

c. 1790

Control of the northern frontier of New Spain by the Spanish military depended greatly on the abilities of the buckskin-and-leather clad presidial soldiers, called *Cueras*. Because of the remoteness of those presidios, most of the *Cueras* had to be recruited from among the inhabitants of that region. Few of them were of pure Spanish blood; most of them were *mestizo* or mixed blood. The *Cueras* were not only isolated by great distances from any of the southern cities, they were under constant threat of Indian attacks. Although inspectors of the presidios came and went, the conditions in those lonely outposts hardly ever improved. Since supplies and replacements seldom arrived, it was difficult to maintain any uniformity in dress. The soldiers had to darn and patch their own clothes, wear homespun garments, replace their regulation capes with native blankets, and make their own leather hats to replace the worn-out black felt hats. According to the Marquis de Rubí, in the report of his inspection tour in 1766, "there was no uniformity in anything, even in the caliber of firearms."

Because of their small numbers and poor equipment, those true frontiersmen never were able to conquer the Indians; however, for the length of the Spanish occupation of the Southwest, they kept the boundaries from receding.

Spanish Frontier Officer

c. 1800

BETWEEN 1800, when Spain became a French satellite under King Carlos IV and First Minister Manuel Godoy, and 1803, when France sold Louisiana to the United States, an effort was made to introduce French fashions into the military forces stationed in the nine Interior Provinces of New Spain.

Because Napoleon was the power behind the throne and actually the indirect originator of all these changes throughout Europe, it is interesting to note that he himself was a mediocre horseman. According to a contemporary "he never used the spur, nor the pressure of the calves to set his horse at a gallop, he started it with a touch of his whip." It is also recorded that he rode with loose reins.

Most closely affected by the new uniform regulations were the regular presidial soldiers. Although some of those new uniforms reached Texas, the troops reluctantly accepted them. The dashing, foreign hussar outfits were worn only for a short time, and before long the homely, undisciplined *Cuera* Dragoons with all their old-fashioned gear, six-inch spur rowels, lance, musket and leather armor were again patrolling the vast and lonely borderlands.

Many officers, either for lack of the proper patterns or considering themselves too far away to comply with army regulations, designed and ordered their own uniforms from the nearest tailor available.

Spanish Texas Field Judge
c. 1800

A COLORFUL SPANIARD of the frontier, known only to a few historians who delve into the forgotten and dusty archives of yesteryear, was the *juez de campo* or field judge. "He functioned as an itinerant official charged with the investigation of thefts, robberies, the carrying away of properties by force, the burning of houses, grain, or other things, whenever the said crimes may be committed in unsettled districts . . . He was also responsible for keeping all records concerning livestock, such as the names of stockmen, locations of ranches and records of brand registrations," according to Professor Sandra L. Myres in *The Ranch in Spanish Texas* (El Paso: Texas Western Press, 1969).

He would be present at rodeos displaying the importance of his position by signaling and shaking his *vara de justicia* — a baton that was traditionally used as a sign of authority — so that the *ganaderos*, big and small, might divide their stock from that owned by the missions.

Mission Indian *Vaquero*

c. 1800

"INDIANS, EVEN IF DESCENDENT from kings, are not allowed to ride horses, under penalty of death." Thus, a Spanish mandate was directed against the natives of New Spain, forbidding them the use of horses, because the Spaniards were fearful and conscious of the advantage the natives would achieve with the knowledge and practice of horsemanship. Although the authorities were very severe in enforcing these laws, there were many times when the Indians, either secretly or through the help of others, found a way or an occasion to get on a horse.

In the missions of the Southwest, especially in California and Texas, some of the *padres* were not only extraordinarily good teachers but also excellent horsemen. Due to the increasing size of their herds and the work that resulted, the missionaries diligently taught the neophytes the essentials of horsemanship. Those early *vaquero* candidates experienced many hard spills before they qualified and so, one might say, they really earned their spurs.

El Señor Cura

c. 1805

FROM THE TIME that Hernán Cortés brought Christianity to Mexico in the sixteenth century, religion has played an important part in the lives of the Mexican people. And throughout the history of Mexico, almost every activity has been regulated or influenced by either the cordial or antagonistic relations between Church and State.

The inevitable conflicts and confrontations between those two institutions began with the servitude and abuse of the natives by some of the newcomers who proved to be greedy and unscrupulous. During that era, the missionaries not only defended the Indians, they also established schools and other institutions in an effort to improve conditions for them.

One of the more unfortunate events that greatly affected the northwestern frontier including Chihuahua, Sonora, Arizona and Baja California, was the expulsion of the Jesuits. Those men of the Church, who had labored long and hard to help the Indian tribes in that region, were expelled and herded out of the country at a predetermined day and hour that was decreed by Carlos III. All of this was done swiftly, unexpectedly and in complete secrecy, thus denying the Jesuits the right to trial, or even to protest. Their schools, which at that time were the best in Mexico, as well as their churches and missions, were abandoned without warning, at the stroke of the royal pen.

Another significant event in which members of the church hierarchy had a very active part was in drafting of the Declaration of Independence from Spain. The most prominent leaders — Miguel Hidalgo y Costilla, José María Morelos y Pavón, and Mariano Matamoros — were Catholic priests.

Mexican *Hacendado*

c. 1810

IN 1825, Don Manuel Eduardo Gorostisa was a confidential agent of the Mexican government, stationed in Brussels, Belgium. While there, he received a petition from two Italian citizens, Claudio Linati and Gaspar Franchini who sought permission to transport a lithography press to Mexico. With permission obtained, monetary help and passports provided, the task of transporting the lithograph press was completed. Two years later Linati returned to Brussels, bearing a passport awarded him by General Guadalupe Victoria, first president of Mexico, and which described Linati as "the introducer of the first lithographic establishment in the Republic of Mexico."

In Brussels, Linati published what some might consider a monumental book titled *Costumes Civiles, Militaires et Religieux du Mexique, Dessinés d'après Nature par C. Linati.* Written in French, the book contains forty-eight lithographic plates in color which depict the civil, military and religious costumes of Mexico. One of the most attractive of these is titled *Hacendado*, in which the attire is a brown and gold riding suit that consists of a short *cotona* with upturned cuffs, and pants that are split on the sides and decorated with gold buttons. The boots have red facings and extremely flared tops, with splits on the outer sides. The subject wears a religious gold medal and a scapular, also a big scarf tied at the neck, and a bandana under the narrow-brimmed, low-crowned hat. Completing the costume is a red sash, a leather belt from which hangs a Spanish rapier and, draped over his shoulder, a silver trimmed, red and blue *manga*, which Linati calls *"espèce de manteau de drap."*

South Texas *Ranchero*

c. 1815

Wherever the spaniards went to extend their frontier, whether to establish a settlement, a mission, a mining town, or a military outpost, they took their cattle and horses, their sheep and goats, even their pigs and chickens with them. Much of the success of their enterprises depended on an ample supply of livestock, which was the backbone of the economy.

The first herd of cattle that crossed Texas territory came through El Paso in 1598 with the Oñate expedition. In South Texas, Captain Alonso de León, the Younger, frontiersman and governor of Coahuila, led an expedition in 1689 to the Neches River in eastern Texas, that brought 200 cattle, 400 horses and 150 mules to that region. The biggest boost given to the cattle industry in Texas was the settlement of the lower Rio Grande region by the group headed by José de Escandón. The efforts and ability of those obstinate *vaqueros* made that country the richest cattle breeding region of North America.

Following the methods and ways of the *hombres* farther south, the *vaqueros* in Texas also used similar equipment. Our *ranchero* has a harness of leather, embroidered and decorated with hemp and silver thread and attached to the saddle. It covers the hind quarters of the horse as low as the mid-thighs, with its lower borders fringed with jingling metal ornaments called *coscojos*. This piece was known as an *anquera* and was developed by the rancheros in imitation of the decorative strap used by the Spanish nobles and called *gualdrapa*.

New Mexico *Comanchero*

c. 1825

COMANCHERO is a word derived from the word "Comanche" and it is defined as a trader who exchanges goods with an Indian tribe.

Necessity was the primary reason why the residents of New Mexico began exchanging goods with the Indians. For almost two centuries, trade and commerce in that region were restricted to the risky and uncertain travel to cities in Mexico that were hundreds of miles away. In order to survive economically, the citizens began trading and exchanging goods with various Indian tribes that were not subject to the Spanish government. There were peaceful trade negotiations between New Mexicans and even the fierce Comanches, which were tolerated by the authorities. In fact, local fairs were held at Pecos and Taos, where homemade cloth, blankets, pottery, knives, beads, and even cornbread were traded to the Indians for buffalo hides, buckskins, or horses and cattle, the later frequently stolen from Mexico or Central Texas. Even captive prisoners were sometimes exchanged for ransom at those fairs.

During the mid-1870s, when the activities of the *Comancheros* were drawing to a close, there were still some traders who would slip away to barter with the Indians at their concealed camps.

"In films and novels today, the *Comancheros* are pictured as renegades and villains of the worst sort," says noted historian Marc Simmons of Cerrillos, New Mexico. "But the fact is, they were simple people, long engaged in legitimate business, who got caught when the times changed and an evil cloud cast its shadow over their activities."

Caporal de Hacienda de Tamaulipas
c. 1825

ONE OF THE MOST IMPORTANT REPOSITORIES of Western art and history is the Gilcrease Institute of Tulsa, Oklahoma. Among the many treasures kept there is a collection of original water color renderings that depict typical Texans and Mexicans during the first quarter of the nineteenth century when Texas was still part of Mexico. Most of the drawings appear to have been done by Lino Sánchez y Tapia, from Matamoros, under the supervision of Jean Louis Berlandier, a young French scientist with the Mexican Boundary Commission. This delegation was set out to explore, study and record the northeast frontier of Mexico in 1826, under the leadership of General Manuel Mier y Terán.

The collection includes a drawing of a *Caporal*, or cowboy foreman, from Tamaulipas. One of the most distinctive features of the rider's costume is the coat, which is a type of *cuera* that is still worn in the states of Guerrero, Michoacán and Baja California. Horsemen in Guerrero and Michoacán who wear the coat are called *cuerudos*. The style was adapted from those worn in *tierra adentro*, or northern Mexico, by soldiers and militiamen in the early eighteenth century, which in turn probably evolved from the military buff coats of the previous century. The coats first appeared in the 1750s in Baja California and the *vaqueros* at the tip of the peninsula still use them.

The Government of Mexico presented to the City of Los Angeles a magnificent equestrian statue of Generalissimo José María Morelos, hero of Mexican independence. Located in Lincoln Park, the statue of Morelos shows him wearing a beautiful *cuera*, or leather coat, from his native state, Michoacán.

Ranchero de Texas
c. 1825

THERE IS A SPANISH SAYING, referring to a stroke of luck or an unexpected event, that goes like this: *Cuando uno menos piensa, salta la liebre,* or "When one least expects it, out jumps the rabbit." While reading some research material, we ran across a letter, written by Reuben Potter in November of 1828, in Matamoros, Mexico. This letter was included in a master's thesis, written in 1939 by James Henry Leach at The University of Texas. Potter was born in 1802 in New Jersey, and in 1827 he went to Mexico to seek his fortune. This excerpt from his letter is a lively description of the riding equipment of the region.

"Their riding gear, of which I have learned the utility, I presume you have never seen in a complete set. The saddle is like those you have seen in Louisiana, high before and behind with wooden stirrups but more ornamental. Suspended from the pommel are the *armas de pelo* as they are called, two goatskins dressed with the hair on, and embroidered at the top. These may be drawn over the knees, to defend from the brambles, or, when it rains, may have the lower corners fastened behind the saddle, to make a more complete covering. Add to these a cloak or Mexican blanket, and one of the broad hats of the country, and you may ride for hours invulnerable to the heaviest rain. At night the *armas* serve you for a bed, and the saddle for a pillow. If you wish to imagine a likeness of myself, when on the road, you have only to suppose me mounted on a swift pacing mule, with all the apparatus above described, and add thereto a Mexican riding dress, a double barrelled gun, a pair of pistols, and a goodly long sword. My servant, as well as the muleteers were armed, though not so completely."

Texas Mexican Presidial Soldier

c. 1825

In 1826, Don Lucas Alamán, Minister of Foreign Affairs of the Republic of Mexico, decided to organize and send an expedition to explore and record the northeast frontier of the country under the name of *Comisión de Límites*. One of the prominent members of the group was José María Sánchez y Tapia, listed as a cartographer and draftsman. From that journey through South and Central Texas came a very interesting set of watercolors, now kept at the Gilcrease Institute in Tulsa, Oklahoma, depicting Texas types of the period. Although José María Sánchez y Tapia was the official draftsman, most of the pictures are signed by Lino Sánchez y Tapia, probably a brother and obviously also an artist.

Among the pictures there is a rendering of a Mexican presidial soldier in a blue uniform, his coat adorned with three rows of silver buttons, a red collar and red cuffs. It is interesting to see the amount of fringed leather articles in his equipment: the sheath of his musket, his back saddle bags, the scabbard of his big knife, his *armas*, chaps, and his leggings. The *cojinillos*, a pair of bags hanging across the front of the saddle, are tooled and embossed in the same manner as the saddle skirts, the *armas*, and the stirrup *tapaderas*.

One item that may seem odd and unmilitary is the tall hat. It shows either the influence of pioneers and merchants arriving from the United States or it was an item required by military regulations. At the beginning of the nineteenth century, tall hats began to appear as parts of military uniforms in several countries: those of the cadets at the Military Academy at West Point, of some British units like the Marine Infantry, and of several regiments in Argentina, Brazil, Portugal, and Peru.

New Mexico *Cibolero*

c. 1825

IT IS A WELL KNOWN FACT that mustangs, longhorns and buffaloes played an important part in the history of the Southwest. Of the three, probably the most important, yet least understood, was the buffalo. For hundreds of years this animal was the main source of sustenance for many Indian tribes throughout a vast area — from Canada to Mexico, as far west as the Rockies, and according to some historians, even as far east as Pennsylvania. In addition to being a source of food, clothing, and shelter, the buffalo fulfilled many other needs of the Indians. The horns and bones were used for implements and ornaments; the hooves were converted into glue; the sinews were made into bowstrings, and buffalo chips served as fuel. Nothing was wasted.

The coming of the Spaniards caused a change in the balance of nature. The Spaniards brought horses, which marked the beginning of the destruction of the buffalo. The Spaniards who became residents of New Mexico began supplementing their diet with buffalo proteins. Through the years, their continual search for additional meat supplies resulted in their forming communal groups to travel as far as the Llano Estacado or the Texas Panhandle region to track down and kill the humped beasts. When out of ammunition, they would use their homemade short lances and, riding horseback, would kill at close range. These hunters called themselves *ciboleros*, derived from the Spanish word for buffalo — *cíbolo*.

Mexican Muleteer

c. 1830

TRAPPERS AND MOUNTAIN MEN who wandered into the Southwest would return to the Mississippi River towns where they often incited the greed and curiosity of their listeners by exclaiming: "Those Spaniards at Santa Fe have more gold and silver than a dog's got fleas, but no place to spend it!" Such provocative reports often resulted in thoughts of how Americans could profit by sending wagon loads of goods cheaper, better and faster than could the merchants from Mexico.

The reported accumulated wealth of New Mexicans was the result of lack of commerce in the province. Since early times, their trade had depended on the very irregular and hazardous trips made by the ox-cart caravans and mule-pack trains from Mexico to Santa Fe. Usually these pack trains consisted of four or five hundred mules and approximately seventy-five muleteers on foot (*arrieros*). Every day, each driver had to gather the animals assigned to him, load them, stay with them, and remove the packs at the end of the day's journey. There were some who took care of the spare animals (*remuda*) and who provided supplies and water for the group as well as feed for the beasts during the rest periods. Two items essential to the muleteer were the *pechera*, a leather apron; and the *tapojo* or blindfold. Because mules are very sensitive and easily scared, they had to be blindfolded every time they were loaded or unloaded. This muleteer is a train master; he is riding the lead mule that has a cowbell hanging from its neck.

Mexican *Ranchero*

c. 1830

There is a story often repeated by Mexican writers concerning the origin of the *silla vaquera*, the Mexican stock saddle. The story claims that the inventor was none other than the second viceroy of New Spain, Don Luis de Velasco. One thing is certain: Velasco was a magnificent horseman and very much interested in livestock raising. Juan Suárez de Peralta, author of a treatise on horsemanship, *Tratado de la jineta y de la brida*, called the viceroy *"un lindo hombre de a caballo,"* a handsome man on horseback. Suárez de Peralta was born in Mexico but his book was published in Spain in 1580.

It is difficult to trace back the beginnings of the *silla vaquera;* however, the following two instances may give us a bit of a hint as to its early use: The lasso was brought from Spain, where the practice of it was part of the exercises of *a la jineta* riding, only that the loop was set at the end of a pole while the end of the lasso was tied to the tail of the horse. This method was taken to Mexico but soon discarded by the innovative native *vaqueros*. Tailing the steers, that is, throwing cattle by the tail, was already common by the middle of the sixteenth century. As both stunts required a good hold on the horse, it is possible that various kinds of *sillas vaqueras* were being used in those early years.

Although the basic element of the saddle, the *fuste*, didn't change much, the coverings, and various accessories contributed to the great variety of shapes and appearance through the centuries. Our *ranchero* shows the last flowering of the *jineta* type saddles. Two originals are at the Los Angeles County Museum, one at the National Museum of History in Mexico City, and two in private collections that we know of.

Mexican *Charro*

c. 1830

DON CARLOS RINCON GALLARDO, Duque de Regla, Marqués de Guadalupe, was a polished gentleman and a splendid horseman. Considered to be the highest authority on contemporary Mexican horsemanship, his book *El Charro Mexicano*, first published in 1939, continues to be considered a "bible" among Mexican horsemen. In the book, the author states: "The Mexican *charro* has his origin from Salamanca, in Spain, where they designate with that name the countryman of that place." No other clarification or explanation is given, yet this statement has been perpetuated exactly as it was written.

Prior to the nineteenth century, the word *charro*, in designation of a horseman, does not appear anywhere. Instead, the words *vaquero, ranchero, hacendado, estanciero, jinete,* and *caballero* were used. *Charro* is a consequence of the process of evolution of the Mexican riding costume. In the late eighteenth century the *rancheros* began to add silver buttons, fringes, tooled buckskin and tassels to their attire. By the first quarter of the nineteenth century, not only was their dress over-decorated but also their horsegear, and so the common people began to call them, in a derogatory manner, *charros*. One of the definitions of *charro* in the Spanish language is: "gaudy, overcharged with ornaments."

Eduardo Pingret, a prominent French artist, did several portraits of important people in the period of 1830 to 1840. He left us some extremely good depictions of *charros* when they began to be called *charros*.

Northern Mexico *Vaquero*

c. 1830

FRANCISCO JAVIER MINA was a dissatisfied young Spanish officer who escaped from his country and, after residing in France, England and the United States, joined forces with Mexican insurgents against Spain, becoming a very prominent leader in the war for Mexican independence. The encounter between Mina and the insurgent chief Don Pedro de Nava is described by Don Niceto de Zamacois in his *Historia de México*, pp. 297-98: "The attire of Nava attracted a lot of attention from Mina and his soldiers. He was dressed in the costume of the rich *rancheros*, which is very striking but quite proper to use on horseback. He had a *jarano* [hat] similar to those used by bullfighters in Spain, but finer and more flexible, with a wide brim and the border decorated in gold and a hat band in silver; a luxurious *jorongo* [mantle] in a beautiful combination of bright colors hanging from his shoulder; a *calzonera* [open-side pants] in rich blue fabric with silver buttons held by a red silk sash with golden tassels; a very fine deer-skin *cotona* [short slip-on jacket] with silver thread embroidery; very showy *botas camperas* [leggings] and expensive spurs with steel jingles that made a very pleasant sound when walking. This is the attire of wealthy people who spend most of their lives on horseback and the one Pedro de Nava wore when he met Francisco Javier Mina."

Mexican General

c. 1840

ANTONIO LOPEZ DE SANTA ANNA helped to free his country from Spanish rule, then later became dictator of Mexico. In the United States, he is best remembered as the general who led his troops in the attack on the Alamo in San Antonio. After Mexico won its independence from Spain in 1821, Santa Anna joined and then deserted several Mexican leaders, always taking the side that he thought would be to his best advantage. Spain tried to reconquer Mexico in 1829 but failed. After overthrowing Emperor Iturbide, Santa Anna made himself President of the Republic of Mexico. When Texas decided to become independent, he led the Mexican army in an effort to prevent Texas from achieving that independence. After a brief success with the campaign, he was defeated by General Sam Houston at the Battle of San Jacinto.

Santa Anna was extremely fond of gambling, horseracing and cockfighting. He was also inclined toward wearing ostentatious and showy uniforms, and his mounts were equipped with flashy horse gear.

Mexican *Ranchero* and His Lady

c. 1840

IN HIS WANDERINGS through Mexico, in the second quarter of the nineteenth century, Carl Nebel, outstanding German lithographer, encountered the great haciendas and the colorful and richly dressed *rancheros*. In describing their life and customs, he noted "Everyone who has to travel on horseback travels this way. The great hat to ward off the rays of the sun, the woolen cloak or 'sarape' to cover the shoulders, the chaps to keep their legs dry, the boots and even the wooden stirrups that hang from a comfortable saddle, all do their job perfectly."

"All," he wrote, "are dressed luxuriously. The only difference is to be found in the varying qualities of the cloth used; the tailoring is the same. Only the poor horse ought not to be quite content with such heavy trappings. Nevertheless, these animals travel twenty to twenty-five leagues without tasting more than a little water."

About the women he said "Mexican women are small, delicate. Their noses and mouths reflect their Indian heritage. Their shoulders are well formed, their breasts and waists, artfully outlined. Their feet are delicate. Young women take care to wear very low heels. Their manner of walk is both graceful and decent at one and the same time. Mexican women are sweet and affable, calm and modest in their conversation. They are frank and natural, unaffected in their treatment even of strangers."

A number of Nebel's drawings lend credence to his remarks about the admirable qualities of Mexican women, several of whom he has captured in different poses, with some of them on horseback.

Californian

c. 1840

IN THE WORDS of Hubert H. Bancroft, who gathered the most accurate information concerning early pastoral California, nothing was more important to the *caballero* than the trappings of his horse. With an ideal environment and all the leisure time in the world, the *caballero's* greatest preoccupation was in maintaining excellent horses and acquiring the finest riding equipment.

When he rode horseback, his legs were encased in beautifully decorated leggings called *gamuzas*. Of these he was very proud, and the method of wrapping his legs was an art in itself. A mantle was worn in cold weather and consisted of an oval piece of woolen cloth, sometimes lined in silk, with an opening in the center for the head. It was similar to, except that it was shorter than, the ones used in Mexico at that time. The garment was both graceful and dignified, and also allowed great freedom of movement.

Born to the saddle, stylish in his trappings, fearless in horsemanship, the *caballero* was one of the most dashing riders the world has ever seen.

Buckskin

c. 1840

TRAPPERS, MOUNTAIN MEN, BUCKSKINS — whichever name one may choose, it signifies those rugged trailblazers who pioneered a new phase of one of the oldest, most complex businesses in North America. For more than two hundred years the fur trade had been all important in that region, because of the great commercial value attached to beaver, mink, marten and otter pelts. Gradually, in the early nineteenth century, the mountain men led America's westward push into northern Mexico. Their long rifles were the forerunners of American rule, and yet, with all New World colonies in revolt, Spain was too busy to understand the significance of the *gringo* visitors.

Several of the mountain men gave their names to history: Jim Baker, Jim Bridger, Kit Carson, Jedediah Smith, Joseph Walker. Typical of these tough wanderers was Joseph Reddeford Walker, who stood out as a kind of beau ideal of the mountain man. Zenas Leonard, one of the chroniclers of the fur trade, summed up his opinion of him in these words: "Mr. Walker was a man well calculated to undertake a business of this kind. He was well hardened to the hardships of the wilderness — understood the character of the Indians very well — was kind and affable to his men, but at the same time at liberty to command without giving offense — and to explore unknown regions was his chief delight."

On November 15, 1821, the governor of New Mexico, Facundo Melgares, warmly received William Becknell as the first merchant to arrive in Santa Fe from Missouri. Becknell, who had been a trapper in the Rockies before becoming a merchant, not only inaugurated the Santa Fe trade, but shaped it significantly.

Mexican *Ranchero*

c. 1840

WE ARE INDEBTED to the many extraordinary artists who visited Mexico in the early part of the nineteenth century, for their valuable inconographic contributions related to the life and people of that country. They include Claudio Linati, Thomas Egerton, Johann Moritz Rugendas, John Phillips, Eduardo Pingret, Léon Gautier, James Walker and Carl Nebel.

Each of them left magnificent visual testimonies of an era that was intensely attractive to aesthetically minded individuals. Probably the most accomplished draftsman of the group was Carl Nebel, a German artist and architectural designer, who lived in the United States but visited Mexico between 1829 and 1834. During the war with Mexico in 1847, he supposedly accompanied U.S. troops in order to sketch war scenes. These were later lithographed and published in a book, and they are considered to be the best non-literary documents of the conflict.

The first time Nebel was in Mexico he produced one of the most beautiful and rare of all Mexican print sets, *Viaje pintoresco y arqueológico sobre la parte mas interesante de la República mexicana.* In this traveling album, Nebel masterfully captured the appealing charm of Mexico and its people. In the opinion of Dr. Justino Fernández, of the Instituto de Investigaciones Estéticas of the National University of Mexico, Nebel had no rival in composing scenes depicting natives, costumes and typical architecture of that period. Exceptionally beautiful are his numerous renditions of *hacendados* and *rancheros* of the early nineteenth century.

Rider from Veracruz
c. 1840

T HE FIRST SETTLEMENT in Mexico, called Villa Rica de la Vera Cruz, was founded by Cortés in 1519, just a short distance north of the present city. In about 1590 it was relocated to a place near the mouth of the river and renamed Nueva Vera Cruz. Then in 1615, Philip III conferred upon it the title and privilege of a city.

The castle of San Juan de Ulúa, set on the island facing the city, was the last foothold of the Spaniards in Mexico. The Spaniards, sent from Havana, remained there until 1825 when they finally surrendered to the Mexican patriots. In 1838 Veracruz was bombarded and taken by the French; then in 1847 it was captured by the Americans under the command of General Winfield Scott. It was surrendered to the allied British, French and Spanish forces in December, 1861, and was not restored to Mexico until 1867.

Veracruz was a main port of entry and was visited by several European artists on different occasions as they traveled to the interior. One of them was the gifted Johann Moritz Rugendas, a German who became fascinated with the color, and landscapes and the picturesqueness of native Mexican costumes. From his very productive work done in Mexico, there is one outstanding rendition of a typical rider from Veracruz that reveals a curious facet of Mexican horsemanship: his rope is tied to the tail of the horse. This indicates that the *vaqueros* in Veracruz were using the same method of holding the roped cattle as were some of the *gauchos* in Argentina and Uruguay.

Supremos Poderes
Presidential Guard
c. 1843

FROM THE FIRST DAY of its independence from Spain, Mexico was beset with problems in organizing and reconstructing her governmental structure. Internal strife, dissensions, and power struggles were to plague the country for decades, thus weakening it and making it an easy target for ambitious and expansionist nations. In spite of much disorganization at the top, Mexico's soldiers conducted themselves bravely and fiercely when compelled to face, at different times, the armies of Spain, France, the United States, and the newly created Republic of Texas. The Mexican soldier of this period, so badly led and shamefully neglected, was on occasion capable of heroic deeds and utmost courage.

During this critical period, continually changing Mexican governments issued different orders and specifications for various types of uniforms. These eventually evolved into the uniform of the Hussar of the Guard of Supreme Powers. This colorful unit was originally a Light Cavalry squadron but on September 1, 1843, they were designated an elite troop that rode at the head of all cavalry formations. They were not officially called Hussars until July 27, 1846. During the war of 1847 they served as the presidential bodyguard, and carried lances with long red and blue, or red pennants.

U. S. Army Mounted Rifles

c. 1847

ONE DAY all Mexicans living north of the Rio Grande awoke to the fact that their nationality had been changed. The end of the war with Mexico automatically made them United States citizens. After taking possession of the land, one of the first things the U. S. Army did was to establish military posts. On November 7, 1848, General Orders No. 58 were issued by the Assistant Adjutant General in Washington, ordering six companies of the Third Regiment of Infantry to "the post opposite El Paso, Mexico." The post which became known as Fort Bliss had its official inception in these orders.

West Texas was then a frontier, where communications were uncertain and at times, unreliable, so the troops that set out for El Paso were ordered to carry "clothing for one year, 60 days subsistence for the march, and rations in addition, for six months."

Late in the following year the troops, consisting of Regimental Headquarters and six companies of the Third Infantry and commanded by Major Jefferson Van Horne, reached their destination. Six days later a military post was established.

This first post at El Paso was situated near the present San Jacinto Plaza. Later it was relocated at what is now the junction of Magoffin Avenue and Willow Street. A third location was near the present Concordia Cemetery; a fourth in the village of Franklin in what is now downtown El Paso, on or near Pioneer Plaza; and a fifth near the present-day Hacienda Restaurant neighborhood. In 1893, the sixth and final location was established on what was called La Noria Mesa. The illustration shows a typical U. S. Army uniform of 1847, worn by The Mounted Rifles.

New Mexico Mountaineer

c. 1850

Looking back on those eighteenth-century New Mexicans who dared to go with their families to live in such isolated places, at that time, as Truchas, Trampas, Jemez or Manzano, we came upon some very interesting and timely observations by contemporary historian Marc Simmons on the subject: "Since the days of the first Spanish settlers, New Mexico has been a place where a fellow could come and spin out his own highly individualistic pattern of living. I recall the many references I have seen in the colonial documents — complaints put forth by Spanish officials against those pioneer New Mexicans who would not conform.

"To the despair of the king's officers, they insisted upon scattering out in the remote countryside instead of congregating in neat, fortified towns as the law required. Governor Fernando de la Concha in 1788 claimed his subjects were 'churlish by nature' and wanted 'to live in perfect freedom' away from the regulating hands of church and state."

We concluded that these *primos* — a term meaning cousins that was affectionately applied among themselves by native New Mexicans — not only were a special breed but also a stubbornly individualistic and fiercely independent group of pioneers.

San Antonian

c. 1850

Don diego de penalosa, who had served as governor of New Mexico in the early 1660s, alerted Spanish authorities to the French menace in East Texas. In 1689 the governor of Coahuila, Alonso de León, was charged with the search for the French and successfully discovered the remains of La Salle's Fort St. Louis at Matagorda Bay. In 1691, on a return trip to East Texas, Domingo Terán de los Ríos, first governor of the Province of Texas, and Father Damián Massanet encamped at a site that the native Payaya Indians called "Yanaguama," or refreshing waters. In need of a way station between New Spain and the East Texas missions, they decided to establish it there. In the words of Father Massanet, "it was the best site in the world, with good and abundant irrigation water, rich lands for pasture, plentiful building stone and excellent timber." Most important of all those factors leading to their decision was the ample water supply. Because they found themselves there on the feast day of Saint Anthony of Padua, they renamed the place San Antonio.

The different settlements at different times — San Antonio de Béxar, San Antonio de Valero, Villa de San Fernando — constitute now the core, the center of the prosperous and beautiful City of San Antonio.

From a photograph of a small, nicely modeled equestrian sculpture of Ernst Dorsch, one of the most celebrated members of the San Antonio Schützenverein, we reconstructed the likeness of a typical San Antonio Anglo in mid-nineteenth century. The model was probably displayed in Mr. Dorsch's Deer Horn Bar at 211 West Commerce Street.

Paso del Norte Travelers
c. 1850

For ALMOST TWO HUNDRED YEARS the principal means of travel for the people of Paso del Norte was either by foot, or riding on the backs of horses, mules, or burros. *Carretas*, or carts, were used primarily for the hauling of firewood, grain, salt, adobes, hides or similar freight. Of the traveling routes, the northbound trail, leading as far as Las Cruces and Doña Ana, was relatively safe. However the southern trail could be used only by large groups of travelers and merchants who assembled for seasonal trips to Chihuahua or farther inward, and who were escorted by presidial soldiers. To the west, the primitive road led to Janos, Casas Grandes, San Buenaventura and as far as the presidios in Sonora and Arizona. It was used mostly for military purposes. The best route for those who wished to visit neighbors and relatives, was along the Rio Grande.

The original names of the settlements were: Nuestra Señora de Guadalupe del Paso del Rio del Norte, (and the presidio, separate from the mission, was called Presidio de Nuestra Señora del Pilar y del Glorioso Señor San José), Real de San Lorenzo, San Antonio de Senecú, Nuestra Señora del Socorro de los Piros, Corpus Christi de la Isleta del Sur, Hacienda de los Tiburcios (now San Elizario). There were other settlements that were abandoned, such as San Francisco de los Sumas, Nuestra Señora de las Caldas, San Pedro de Alcántara, San José, and Real del Santísimo Sacramento de los Tiguas.

New Mexico Horseman

c. 1850

ALTHOUGH MODERN NEW MEXICO occupies a very prominent place in the art world, in earlier times, during the Spanish and Mexican periods the practice of the arts was lamentably delegated to a few *santeros* who would carve religious images or paint them on wooden boards and buffalo hides. For this reason it is extremely difficult to find any graphic or pictorial material concerning early New Mexican types. One of the rare depictions of a New Mexican *caballero* is a watercolor kept at the Bancroft Library in California, possibly done by Alexander Barclay. It shows a horseman of the middle nineteenth century in full attire. The picture coincides with a description given by Robert M. Denhart in his exceptional book *The Horse of the Americas*: "The New Mexican developed a riding costume almost unique, the clothes of the early California *caballeros* alone comparable to it. The outfit was always topped by a *sombrero* — a low crowned hat with a wide brim — covered with oilcloth and encircled by a hat band made of tinsel cord nearly an inch in diameter. The jacket, or *chaqueta*, was marvelously embroidered, decorated with braid and barrel buttons. For trousers they wore a peculiarly shaped garment called *calzoneras* with the outer part of the legs open from hip to ankle — the border set with twinkling filigree buttons, and the whole fantastically trimmed with tinsel lace and cords. The leggings, or *botas*, whose nearest relatives are perhaps those leggings worn by the bandits of old Italy, were made of embossed leather, embroidered with fancy silk and tinsel thread and bound to the knee with curiously tasseled garters. A *sarape saltillero*, or fancy blanket, completed the outfit. . . ."

Paso del Norte Roper

c. 1850

WHEN DEALING WITH EVENTS and happenings of our past we must keep in mind that for more than two hundred years the Paso del Norte region was part of New Mexico and as a result, our history is interwoven with and intimately related to the history of our neighboring state. During the Spanish colonial period, the families from El Paso and Mesilla valleys had much in common with those of the Rio Arriba settlements — same institutions, same ancestral roots, same customs, same problems. War and political disturbances eventually divided the land among three states and two countries.

New Mexican horsemen of the early nineteenth century have been praised by some historians for their superb horsemanship and the beauty of their riding equipment, ignoring the fact that the same honor could have been applied to the *vaqueros* of Paso del Norte, who were equal to if not better than their northern *compadres*.

The *Paseños* on occasion would join groups from Mesilla and Las Cruces and go buffalo hunting on the eastern plains around the Texas Panhandle. This was a task that demanded skill, horsemanship and courage.

A self-sufficient individual, the *vaquero*, could braid his own rope, build his own saddle and his *chaparreras*, in addition to handling cattle and taming wild horses. It was, however, in throwing the lasso — an instrument of twisted hide or horsehair — that he found the diversion he most enjoyed.

Californian

c. 1855

THERE MUST BE OTHERS, but Hernando Villa, Don Perceval, Stan Galli and Jo Mora have devoted much of their lives to portraying and exalting the colorful California *caballeros*. With keen vision, great love and understanding they have accumulated with their work the best possible pictorial record on the life and the people when the state was young. One of Jo Mora's lifelong interests was the California *vaqueros*, that hearty breed of missionary-trained horsemen who tended the immense mission herds for eighty years before the Texas cowboys appeared on the national scene. Besides being a renowned sculptor and prolific illustrator, Mora was the author of several books. In his *Californios* he gives a very lively description of an early caballero: "The American vaquero or cowboy — call him what you will — first rode his pony into Alta California and what was later to be our own United States on May 14, 1769. A kerchief was bound about his head, atop which, at a very rakish, arrogant angle sat a trail-worn, weather-beaten hat, wide of brim, low of crown, held in place by a *barbiquejo* (chin strap) that extended just below the lower lip. His unkempt black beard scraggled over his jowls, and his long black hair dangled down his back to a little below the line of his shoulders. His ample colonial shirt was soiled and torn, and a flash of brown shoulder could usually be seen through a recent tear. His short pants, reaching to his knees, buttoned up the sides, and were open for six inches or so at the bottom. Long drawers (which were once white) showed wrinkles at the knees and were folded into wrapped leather *botas*. He wore a rough pair of buckskin shoes with leather soles and low heels, to which were strapped a pair of large and rusty iron spurs."

Comanche Warrior

c. 1860

O F ALL THE HARDSHIPS endured by the settlers of the borderlands, the greatest were the constant Indian raids. The small, isolated communities had few defenses against the daring attacks, for the Indians' audacious hit-and-run methods were difficult to counter successfully. The warriors would strike, then quickly retreat to such distances that pursuit was difficult if not impossible. On the occasions when the pursuers managed to keep up with them, the Indians would disband and flee separately in all directions.

Taking all this into account, the report dated 1786 from Commandant General Jacobo Ugarte y Loyola, who was himself an Indian fighter, strikes a curious note. The report is of his own words, delivered in the Indians' own language, to a delegation of Comanches who had come to Chihuahua City to confirm a peace treaty. The Commandant had this to say:

"All of these Indians are robust, good looking and extremely happy. Their faces show forth the martial, frank and generous character that distinguishes this nation from the others from this frontier. Their dress is decent, fashioned from buffalo skins they provide themselves. They paint their faces with red ochre and other earths, highlighting their eyelids with vermillion. They love adornments and sport them especially in their hair which they wear braided and intertwined with beads..."

George Catlin, noted nineteenth-century American painter who for a time lived among the Comanches, called them "the most extraordinary horsemen that I have seen yet in all my travels."

Santa Fe Trail Wagonmaster

c. 1860

DURING THE TIME when covered wagons and freighters made their runs on the Oregon and the Santa Fe Trails, the wagonmaster was of prime importance in the control and management of the convoy.

In many ways, wagon freighting resembled a military operation. Each wagon train, called an "outfit," was led by a wagonmaster, whose authority over his men equaled that of a commanding officer. He patroled the train and also rode ahead of it. If the train was ox-drawn, he was responsible for the herd of extra animals that accompanied the train, used as replacements for those that became injured or lame.

Of the various companies and entrepreneurs in the wagon train business, the firm of Russell, Majors & Waddell became so synonymous with freighting that it sometimes seemed as if that firm had invented the idea. Alexander Majors, the trailwise partner of Russell and Waddell, issued to every employee of the freighting company a pair of Colt revolvers for defense against the Indians. He also gave them a Bible for defense against "moral contaminators." And to the wagonmaster he handed a printed sheet with a set of twenty "Instructions to Wagon-Masters and all Employees connected with our Train," that had to be followed to the letter.

Chinaco

c. 1860

ALTHOUGH some politically-bent historians have idealized them unnecessarily, the *chinacos* were actually nothing more than the *rancheros* and cowboys who fought with the Republican party of Mexico against French intervention. On the opposing side was the Conservative party, headed by General Miguel Miramón, which consisted of *rancheros* who wore the same type of clothes, were outfitted with the same types of weapons and horsegear, and who joined him to fight for what they thought was a just cause. Yet when their attire, their accouterments and their deeds are discussed by those historians, it is the *chinacos* who are exalted and given the majority of credit. Their dress was the typical riding costume of that period, and neither side had a monopoly on the style. The name *chinacos* had a political implication as opposed to that of their adversaries who were called by the unflattering term of *mochos*.

Most of these men, by their very nature and upbringing, were ideal cavalrymen — cunning, rough and rugged outdoorsmen who had spent most of their lives astride horses.

The Pony Express

c. 1861

THE PONY EXPRESS was established as a temporary means of transporting the United States mail to and from the midwest to California. The formal order was signed by E.S. Childs, Postmaster General, on March 12, 1861 and it specified the route that was to be followed from St. Joseph, Missouri, or Atchison, Kansas, to Placerville, California. It applied to the continuance of operations only until the completion of the Overland Telegraph lines. With their completion, on October 20, 1861, the Pony Express route was discontinued.

A final salute, resembling a eulogy, was given to the Pony Express by a Mr. McClatchy, editor of the *Sacramento Bee* newspaper in California, on October 26, 1861. It read:

"Farewell, Pony: Our little friend, the Pony, is to run no more. 'Stop it' is the order that has been issued by those in authority. Farewell and forever, thou staunch, wilderness-overcoming, swift-footed messenger. For the good thou hast done we praise thee; and, having run thy race, and accomplished all that was hoped for and expected, we can part with thy services without regret, because, and only because, in the progress of the age, in the advance of science and by the enterprise of the capital, thou hast been superseded by a more subtle, active, but no more faithful public servant. Thou wert the pioneer of a continent in the rapid transmission of intelligence between its peoples and hast dragged in thy train the lightning itself, which in good time will be followed by steam communication by rail...

"...This is no disgrace for flesh and blood cannot always war against the elements. Rest, then, in peace; for thou hast run thy race, thou hast followed thy course, thou hast done the work that was given thee to do."

Hacendado

c. 1865

EMPEROR MAXIMILIAN, ever conscious of the good image he wished to present to the Mexican people, exhibited great interest in their customs and beliefs. He even dressed in Mexican attire for his early morning rides. Gifted with artistic talent and a creative mind, he designed Mexico City's beautiful boulevard that extends from Alameda Park to Chapultepec. The boulevard was named Paseo del Emperador in his honor, however after his downfall, it was renamed Paseo de la Reforma. He designed the court's china service, also coins, medals and carriages. In addition, he designed uniforms for the various branches of his imperial army and for the honor guard of Empress Carlotta. And for himself, he designed a black *charro* suit and ordered it to be made of the finest fabric. Until then, black had never before been used for riding costumes. Following Maximilian's lead, the aristocrats quickly adopted the new fashion for themselves.

The use of black, originated by Maximilian, still survives, and today's *charros* are, on formal occasions, dressed in attire that is very similar to that which was conceived long ago by the ill-fated European prince.

U.S. Army Buffalo Soldier

c. 1870

THE ARMY that emerged from the Civil War tamed the last frontiers of the Southwest and became the frontier army of the West. Postwar Indian combat and exploration kept the soldiers active. Protecting new settlements, guarding the building of railroads, watching over trails and communications were just a few of the functions performed by the army. New forts were created as bases for supplies and operations. Fort Stockton, Fort Quitman and particularly Fort Davis, north of the Big Bend region, were garrisoned by the colorful "Buffalo Soldier," a nickname given by the Indians to Negroes in military service.

Many of the white officers in command of those soldiers made no secret of their contempt towards them. Discrimination ran rampant; supplies, equipment, living quarters and assignments were often detoured or withheld. In spite of humiliations and unfair treatment, the Buffalo Soldiers compiled outstanding records of service in action.

For several years the 9th and 10th Cavalry as well as the 24th and 25th Infantry were composed of black soldiers whose uniformed appearance added a striking and picturesque note to our desert landscape. Ironically, they were engaged in the pursuit and extermination of other minorities who did not willingly relinquish their freedom or their rights.

Cowboy of the Cattle Trails
c. 1870

ONE OF THE MOST EXCITING CHAPTERS in American history concerns the cattle drives that originated in Texas just after the Civil War. Although the era of cattle trailing was comparatively brief, its legacy of legends and lore established permanently the image of the American cowboy.

Of the many routes and cattle paths along which the beasts were driven northward, the Chisholm Trail was the best known and most extensively used. The convenience of the streams that crossed it, and the abundant pasturage along the way made this the best course of travel for the big longhorn herds. What an experience it must have been to watch those enormous herds of cattle moving north, bawling, grunting, munching the lush grass and raising a curtain of dust with their hooves, to see the cowpunchers, riding at each side of the cattle, and waving their hats, shouting curses, snapping their long rawhide whips or whistling shrilly at the steady but slow-moving herd whose numbers seemed to fill up the entire horizon.

The last stop for the cattle drive was usually Abilene, Kansas, which was at that time the bovine metropolis of the West. From there the cattle were distributed to various Eastern points. Those cattle trails were the genesis of modern ranching, and they helped to immortalize the cowboy as an American legend.

Apache Lookout

c. 1870

THE APACHES lived mostly in the southwestern regions of the country, in what became the states of New Mexico and Arizona, and in the northern areas of the Mexican States of Sonora, Chihuahua and Coahuila. At one time the Apaches, along with the Comanches, were considered to be the fiercest and most savage warriors of all the tribes in the Southwest. Their acquisition of horses from the Spaniards enabled them to become exceptional horsemen, and also gave them the mobility to conduct raids on their peaceful neighbors for the purpose of robbing them of food, horses, sheep, and even taking their women and children as captives. During the Spanish and Mexican period, they were a constant menace to the populated areas of the borderlands. It was only when the cavalry of the U.S. Army officially moved in and fought them that, in 1886, the tribes surrendered.

Geronimo, Victorio and Cochise were three of their leaders during the Indian wars. Geronimo was considered the most skillful and cunning of the Indian warriors. When he surrendered to General Nelson A. Miles, he was sent to Florida with the promise that he would be allowed to live with his wife and children. However the climate didn't agree with him, so he was sent to Fort Sill, Oklahoma, where he died in 1909.

Many Apaches enlisted with the U.S. Army and became trusty and reliable scouts.

Billy the Kid

c. 1880

FOLLOWING THE CIVIL WAR, gunslingers and desperados were both prevalent and active throughout the West, and the most notorious of them were dead by the early 1890s. It was during a span of only a quarter of a century or less that train and stagecoach robberies, bank holdups, gunfights, hangings, and accompanying reward posters played such a dramatic and colorful role.

One whose reputation and exploits were to endure throughout the decades to come was Billy the Kid. The amount of written and printed material about his life has not only increased his stature as a folk hero, it has also generated a fascination for his bloodstained adventures that verges on morbid interest. For a while, during which Billy the Kid participated in several shootouts, he was not given undue notoriety. However during the Lincoln County War, in which occurred the most notable range fighting in the state of New Mexico, he barely escaped from being burned alive. It was this incident that thrust him into the limelight. From then on, his infamous reputation seemed to increase as fast as the notches on his murderous six-shooter. Some writers claim that he provided "lead passports to eternity" to at least a dozen persons, while others either add to or subtract from that total. True to his name, the Kid died young, at the hand of Pat Garrett, on the eve of July 14, 1881, at Fort Sumner.

During his wanderings, whether chasing his prey at full speed or dodging a shower of bullets from behind, he depended greatly on the speed and agility of his steed.

Texas Gunfighter
c. 1880

AFTER THE CIVIL WAR, the country quickly regained its confidence, optimism and spirit of progress. With communications greatly improved, the renewed westward movement brought people from different countries, cultures, and occupations. There were merchants, lawyers, carpenters, harlots, gamblers, preachers, and gunfighters.

The gunfighter of those days has been the source of an infinite amount of folklore and legend. His ability to handle a six-shooter, and the incredible speed of his draw, have been greatly embellished and at times, even exaggerated.

In a land and time where most of the population was armed, few men could be singled out as exceptionally talented in the use of firearms. This skill had a market value, for it could be employed in the enforcement of law, or hired for purposes that ranged all the way from escorting a stagecoach run, to outright murder. It was an unwritten law in those days that whoever was first to draw his gun was liable for the consequences of a gunfight. The gunfighter, with his accurate marksmanship and superior swiftness of draw, had a legal excuse for manslaughter, and usually claimed self defense in causing the demise of his victim.

The basic and absolutely necessary equipment of the gunfighter consisted of his gun and a good horse.

West Texas Circuit Rider

c. 1880

W HEN AMERICA WAS YOUNG, it was difficult for the scattered communities to receive religious instruction. Francis Asbury, a most devout follower of the teachings of John Wesley, was an early Methodist missionary to the New England colonies. When he stepped off the boat in Philadelphia in 1771, Asbury discovered that there were but a thousand members of the church throughout all the settlements in the New World. The young man soon decided that the only hope for expansion of the Methodist movement lay in "the circulation of preachers." He then became the first circuit rider, traveling on horseback from one settlement to another, shaking hands, singing religious hymns, and spreading the "Good News."

Soon after, preachers from other denominations emulated him and thus created a practice that spread as far and as fast as the frontier advanced.

In nineteenth-century Texas it was not uncommon to encounter these itinerant, devoted gentlemen of the cloth, leading in prayer such diverse groups of people as simple, honest farmers or rowdy crowds of rangehands.

West Texas Sheriff

c. 1880

THE RAPID GROWTH of the towns on the Western frontier created social conditions that were unique in the newly acquired lands. In addition to the different cultures, religions and customs trying to cohabit in a peaceful and progressive manner, there was disorder and violence committed by undisciplined and untamed adventurers. All of these, combined with the practices of partitioning and land-grabbing, created tremendous problems for the honest, hardworking pioneers and the law enforcement agencies.

In addition to the existing social conditions, there was the weakness of the law itself that was not designed to fit either the needs of such an untamed land, or to be interpreted in a variety of foreign languages. Given the situation as it was, few individuals wanted a career in law enforcement, therefore it was often difficult to find a man who would wear the tin badge and stand up to the outlaws. Some of those who did take on the job were either cowards or easy to bribe. Since there was usually a lack of law enforcement personnel, makeshift posses were often formed on the spot and deputized by a sheriff.

Considering all these difficulties, it is somewhat surprising that frontier justice could produce so many distinguished and outstanding law enforcers.

Lawman West of the Pecos
c. 1880

THE WESTERNMOST SPOT IN TEXAS is known today as El Paso, and there could be no better backdrop for a Lawman West of the Pecos than that city when it, and the West, were young. Frederick A. Ober, a writer from Massachusetts who "pasó por aqúi" in 1882, included some of his personal experiences in his book *Travels in Mexico*. The following selected paragraphs give his view and evaluation of El Paso during his visit in the latter part of the 19th century.

". . . descended to the 'office,' registered and was assigned a room at the 'Central,' then the largest hotel in town, and by all odds the dirtiest hotel in the State, though fairly served." He continues: "The town — whose inhabitants will doubtless be mortally offended because I do not call it a city — is about half a mile across, and situated in the centre of a verdureless, mud-colored plain with a semicircle of gravelly hills on one side and the Rio Grande on another.

"Its buildings are mainly new, as houses of wood and brick are fast replacing the old adobe hovels; there are several hotels, numerous large and well-supplied stores, two banks, many good residences going up in the suburbs and plenty of room for expansion. There are several newspapers here, one of which, *The Times*, displays energy, ability and enterprise.

"There are abundant indications that El Paso will grow to the proportions of a great and perhaps attractive city as it has an advantageous situation, nearly four thousand feet above sea level and is entered by several great railroads.

"Across the river from El Paso is Paso del Norte, an unpretentious mud village, which is content to remain so, if those restless Americans from over the Border will only allow it to."

Hacendado Porfiriano
c. 1880

THE LAST QUARTER of the nineteenth century is considered to be the golden era of the *charro* by José Alvarez del Villar, foremost contemporary authority on Mexican horsemanship.

The successful transformation of Mexico from the chaos of former administrations to a nation with stability and peace was the work of Porfirio Díaz in the early years of his long tenure as president of the republic. The *latifundistas*, or big landed estate owners, were greatly favored by the government. Under its system, it was not uncommon for many of them to be appointed state governors or heads of big corporations. Don Luis Terrazas, General Miguel Ahumada and Enrique C. Creel, all from Chihuahua, were prime examples. For many years, Don Luis Terrazas owned almost half of the state of Chihuahua.

It became fashionable for these *hacendados* to send their sons to European colleges, especially in England and France. On their return, these indolent "educated" youngsters showed more interest in transplanting the refinement, the charm, and the fashion trends of the Old World to their homeland than utilizing any knowledge they had acquired. Their ideas of fashion greatly influenced the change in national riding attire.

Tight-fitting, carefully tailored trousers took the place of the loose, open *calzoneras*. The jackets became lavishly decorated with buckskin cut work and gold and silver thread. Most radically changed were the hat styles, which acquired a very unique conical shape with an extremely wide and richly decorated brim.

This group of wealthy innovators is nostalgically remembered as the *Vieja Guardia*, or the Old Guard.

Texas Ranger

c. 1880

IN AMERICAN HISTORY, the most feared and famed organization of frontier fighters for law and order was undoubtedly the Texas Rangers. The Rangers were described as "a special body of irregular troops." As such, they were set apart from the regular Army of Texas, as well as from the state's volunteer militia. Although subject to military discipline, the Ranger carried no flag, wore neither badge, insignia nor symbol of rank, and did not wear an official uniform. He was required to furnish his own weapons and his own mount. He seems to have appeared almost always as the "good guy" in his fight against the foes, whether Indians, Anglo troublemakers, or Mexicans. His admirers believed that he never killed a man unless he had to, although he had to kill many men in the line of duty. In most historical and fictional accounts, he usually appears as the winner, regardless of whether the odds were three to one or a dozen to one, all of which emphasized his motto, "One riot, one Ranger."

Mexican *Rurales* Corps

c. 1880

To repel raids by Indians and outlaws, the Mexican landowners of the eighteenth and nineteenth centuries formed semi-military units of mounted and armed ranchhands. This was a revival of the sixteenth-century *Santa Hermandad* (Holy Brotherhood), a rural constabulary against lawless elements. These units were confirmed in 1710 by the king of Spain, and later functioned as the *Acordada,* a vigilante-style drumhead court. Their first official designation as *Rurales* appears in a January 17, 1842 decree by Santa Anna, to the effect that "on principal ranches, cavalry companies shall be formed and named *Rurales,* under control of the ranch owners, but in armed actions subject to the Military Commandancy." Re-established in 1861 as four corps of rural state police, they were elevated to federal status in 1869, and in 1880 emerged as a militarized, uniformed and armed corps that served for thirty years as the reliable stormtroopers of President Porfirio Díaz. Following the principle that it takes a thief to catch a thief, Díaz not infrequently recruited the best of Mexico's outlaws into the ranks of this revitalized force. Their uniforms were a version of the national riding costume, consisting of gray *charro* suits trimmed with white piping, and striped insignia.

Bandido in Ambush

c. 1890

To eliminate banditry throughout Mexico, President Porfirio Díaz organized the bandits into a police force whose purpose was to police other bandits. It worked extraordinarily well. Those he selected as the core of the group, in turn invited guerrilla groups who had been terrorizing certain areas, to join the *Acordada*, as the corps of *rurales* was sometimes called. Their pay was meager and they did prey on those outlaws who did not join up with them. Most of the members of the *Acordada* remained bandits, but with better advantage, since they were now under cover of the law. With the bandits at his disposal, plus a well trained army and a network of spies, Porfirio Díaz was able to remain in power for almost four decades. These colorful troopers, who were at their best when participating in the 16th of September yearly parades, retained their official status until 1913. Faithful to the end of the doomed regime, the *Acordada* was disbanded when the Federals lost out to the revolutionaries.

Mexican Border Patrol

c. 1890

At the turn of the century, a unique group of law enforcement officers was created by the Mexican government to counteract and control the smuggling of goods and products from the United States. It was organized in a manner similar to that of the *rurales* — horse equipment, arms and typical Mexican riding suits, except that the latter were dark blue. Their official name was *Guardias Fiscales de la Frontera*, or Border Customs Patrol, and they patrolled, on horseback, the Mexican border. They carried pistols in swiveling open holsters, attached to a belt, that could be discharged without unholstering the weapons. They also had Belgian carbines with cylinders like those in revolvers. The customary wearing of long beards gave most of the members a quaint and fierce-looking appearance that was probably intended to be a deterrent to contrabandists.

Ranchero de Chihuahua

c. 1900

URING THE LATE 1880s, noted Western artist Frederic Remington passed through El Paso enroute to a sketching trip in Mexico. While in Chihuahua, Mexico, he visited the Babícora Ranch at the foothills of the Sierra Madre where he watched the Mexican *vaqueros* at their work. These are exerpts from his keen observations.

"My imagination had never pictured before anything so wild as these leather-clad *vaqueros*. They were clad in terracota buckskin, elaborately trimmed with white leather, and around their lower legs were heavy cowhides as a sort of legging. They were fully armed, and with their jingling spurs, their flapping ropes and buckskin strings, and with their gay *serapes* tied behind their saddles, they were as impressive a cavalcade of desert-scampers as it has been my fortune to see. One who finds pleasure in action can here see the most surprising manifestations of it. Here one sees the matchless horsemanship of the 'punchers.' Their little ponies, trained to the business, respond to the slightest pressure.

"A 'puncher' buys nothing but his gorgeous buckskin clothes, and his big silver-mounted straw hat, his spurs, his *riata* and his *cincha* rings. He makes his *teguas* or buckskin boots, his heavy leggings, his saddle and the *patron* furnishes his arms.

"Such is the life of the *vaquero* — a brave fellow — a fatalist with less wants than the pony he rides, a rather thoughtless man who lacks many virtues, but when he mounts his horse or casts his *riata*, all men must bow and call him master."

Texas Cowboy

c. 1900

No MORE FORCEFUL AND ATTRACTIVE CHARACTER has emerged from the American West than the cowboy. The amount of literature and art devoted to him surpasses that dedicated to any other type of folk hero. The artists who have depicted him, yesterday and today, here and abroad, can be counted in the thousands. He has been both falsely represented and genuinely portrayed in books and movies. Often he has written his own story; at other times those using information from other sources have profited from yet another depiction of the cowboy's way of life. His lingo, his songs, his philosophy, his mannerisms, his manner of speech, his equipment — everything about him has been subjected to analysis by generations of writers, and no doubt his story will be repeated and retold in the future. His place in the history and folklore of the West will endure forever.

Charro
Turn of the Century

In THE DECADE preceding the outbreak of the Mexican revolution of 1910, the *charro* suit had evolved into a distinctive and streamlined design. Done in costly fabrics and discreetly adorned with gold and silver, it was extensively used by rich *hacendados* in everyday activities as well as formal occasions.

And so it was when the social conflict began. The contenders took the men from the North and sent them to the South, and those from the Isthmus to the frontier that bordered the United States. The cultivated fields were turned into battlegrounds; the *vaquero* became a soldier, as did the farmhand; horses and saddles were battle equipment and the entire nation became a vast military drilling ground that involved all Mexicans.

The big cattle herds were booty for both sides and in this turmoil the *charros* lost their identity, with only a few of the leaders here and there clinging to the traditional garb. The big *hacendados* either fled with their families to another country or relocated in the big cities. The entire nation hovered on the brink of ruin, and the *charros* — and what they stood for — faded into near-oblivion.

But then, in 1921, the National Association of Charros was formed for the purpose of reinstating, preserving, maintaining and guarding the centuries-old equestrian traditions of the country. Spearheading this reformation was Ramón Cosío González, a distinguished lawyer from Tamaulipas.

President Díaz' Honor Guard

c. 1909

A<small>N EVENT</small> of great historical significance took place in El Paso on October 16, 1908. President William H. Taft of the United States, and President Porfirio Díaz of Mexico met each other at the boundary line between the two countries for an unprecedented visit, after an exchange of courtesies and protocol. Virginia Turner, *El Paso Herald Post* newspaperwoman, described the event in retrospect in one of her columns.

"The Mexican president was escorted with dignity, pomp, guards and a band playing the Mexican National Anthem, to a carriage in which he rode to the boundary where a 21-gun salute was fired by American batteries. He was escorted to San Jacinto Plaza, and then to the Chamber of Commerce where the two presidents met and light refreshments were served.

"Díaz left at 11:30 a.m. and returned to Juarez. Taft left the Chamber and rode to Juarez where he was received with great ceremony by Díaz and Mexican officials, followed by a reception. On return to El Paso, Taft led a military and civic parade through downtown to a reviewing stand at the entrance of Cleveland Square..."

In 1903, President Díaz, greatly impressed with the showmanship of the rising German army, appointed a commission to change the uniform of his soldiers, imitating the military design of the Prussians. During Díaz' visit to El Paso, observers recognized the Teutonic influence when they saw the resplendent peaked helmets with flowing silk plumes that were worn by his Presidential Guard.

Villista

c. 1913

FOR MORE THAN THIRTY YEARS President Porfirio Díaz gave Mexico stability, peace, order and progress, but eventually his stagnant regime resulted in an intolerable situation for the populace. His close-knit bureaucracy encouraged and practiced favoritism, abuse of power, and nepotism. This in turn produced a lack of political freedom and allowed the rich to become richer while the poor became poorer.

For the Mexican peasants, the situation became more hopeless with every passing year, as it was for Díaz' political opponents. It was through desperate efforts by both the lower classes and the politicians who opposed him that the Díaz government was finally overthrown. However this did not solve the problems, for the struggle for power continued among many of the resulting rival factions.

Without understanding the real meaning or the consequences of the overthrow, the peasants joined in the Revolution. Their motives were based on hope and the desire to improve their living conditions, and their dreams were of a brighter future and a better tomorrow. Their dull, unvarying existence was devoid of earthly pleasures; they lacked education and opportunity, and they were perennially embroiled in debts to their respective landlords. The peasants believed that their only chance of freedom was to face the danger of being perforated by enemy bullets.